PTSD and Addiction

TITLES IN THE HAZELDEN PROFESSIONAL LIBRARY

Brief Intervention

A Clinician's Guide to Methamphetamine

Drug Testing in Correctional Settings: Guidelines for Effective Use

Drug Testing in Schools: Guidelines for Effective Use

Drug Testing in Treatment Settings: Guidelines for Effective Use

Hierarchy of Recovery: From Abstinence to Self-Actualization

Motivational Interviewing and Stages of Change: Integrating Best Practices for Substance Abuse Professionals

PTSD and Addiction: A Practical Guide for Clinicians and Counselors

Stages of Change and Addiction

Starting a Recovery School: A How to Manual

Teen-Intervene: Using Brief Intervention with Substance-Abusing Adolescents

Time-Effective Treatment: A Manual for Substance Abuse Professionals

The Twelve-Step Facilitation Handbook: A Systematic Approach to Recovery from Substance Dependence

PTSD and Addiction

A Practical Guide for Clinicians and Counselors

Jerry A. Boriskin, Ph.D.

HAZELDEN®

Hazelden
Center City, Minnesota 55012-0176

1-800-328-9000
1-651-213-4590 (Fax)
www.hazelden.org

13-digit ISBN: 978-1-59285-152-2

Library of Congress Cataloging-in-Publication Data

Boriskin, Jerry A.
PTSD and addiction : a practical guide for clinicians and counselors / Jerry A. Boriskin.
p. ; cm. — (Hazelden professional library)
Includes bibliographical references and index.
ISBN 1-59285-152-5 (softcover)
1. Dual diagnosis—Treatment. 2. Post-traumatic stress disorder—Complications. 3. Dual diagnois—Patients—Rehabilitation. 4. Twelve-step programs. I. Title: Post-traumatic stress disorder and addiction. II. Title. III. Series.
[DNLM: 1. Stress Disorders, Post-Traumatic—complications. 2. Substance-Related Disorders—complications. 3. Diagnosis, Dual (Psychiatry) WM 170 B734p 2004]
RC564.68.B676 2004
616.85'21—dc22

2004042377

Editor's Note

"Marines Call It That 2,000 Yard Stare" by Tom Lea is printed courtesy of the National Museum of the U.S. Army, Army Art Collection.

All the stories in this book are based on actual experiences. The names and details have been changed to protect the privacy of the people involved. In some cases, composites have been created.

This book is not intended as a substitute for the advice of physicians and mental health professionals. The reader should consult these professionals in matters relating to his or her health.

08 07 06 05 04 6 5 4 3 2 1

Cover design by Theresa Gedig
Interior design by Kinne Design
Typesetting by Stanton Publication Services, Inc.

To the staff at Advanced Recovery Center
who translated my vision into being,
especially Cyndy Bourke, R.N., M.Ed., C.S.,
an indescribable talent, co-founder, and administrator

To the clients—past, current, and future—
whose enlightenment is a blessing to witness

And to Wendy, the love of this incarnation and all of eternity

CONTENTS

ACKNOWLEDGMENTS

Simply stated, this book is part of a personal journey that I hope will provide clarity, meaning, and deserved richness to those suffering from trauma-related disorders in concert with addiction.

A short list of those who provided support, feedback, guidance, and care:

Cookie Anderson
Claudia Black
Bill Bogart
Madeline Bryson
Don Catherall
Lynn Eggers
Don Elverd
Sid Farrar
Claude and Sandra Foster
William Friedrich
Jackie Fritz
Trish Gaffney
Stan Grice
Judy Ham
Jerry Herbst
Jeff Hoch
Mark Houston
Debra and Jeff Jay
Caryl Keating
Bruce Larson
Mary Merchant
Gordon Morris and staff
Mark Mulvihill
Deborah Parker
Jerry Rudd
Stephanie Shore
Richard Solly
Rose and Jack Stillson
Sharon Stillson
William Weitz
Barbara Zuckerman

INTRODUCTION

It is better to be lucky than rich or smart, or that is what my grandmother used to say. Some people are lucky enough to go through the predictable tragedies of life relatively unscathed. Others seem to suffer greater trauma in those same tragedies, or they collide with unimaginable circumstances. During recent decades, our perception of how powerful events affect individuals and their connection to the disease of addiction has changed dramatically. This has modified how we deal with the consequences of "bad luck" and traumatic events. We used to believe that people who "cracked under pressure" were defective, undisciplined, morally weak, or poorly trained. Our thinking paralleled the way we thought about addiction less than a century ago.

To some extent, we are all survivors. We all know what it is like to be lonely, tired, frightened, and hurt. However, not everyone develops a trauma-related disorder. While we think we know about the effects of trauma and loss, methodical study of the connection between events, behaviors, and addiction has taken place only in the last thirty years. Many questions have been answered, but new questions continue to emerge. We have learned this: Trauma is a huge factor in the development of many conditions—conditions that were once thought to develop independent of trauma. Today's clinician must know more than clinicians a generation ago. Clinicians trained in addictive disorders have little knowledge about trauma-based phenomena. Similarly, experts in trauma tend to have little knowledge about addictive disorders. Today's complex clients require an understanding of both fields. The goal of this book is to teach some of the fundamentals and facilitate the much-needed convergence of two conceptual and clinical models.

Readers will not become trauma or addiction experts, but they will begin to understand how these two conditions affect clients who relapse and who do not respond to approaches that seem to work for others. The reader will see the missing link: the effect of tragic events on the clients who now seek our services. We no longer live in an era of one condition or another. In our stressful and ever-changing world, we are seeing more complex blends of environmental factors, genetics, addiction, and psychological disorders. What clinicians see or fail to see can profoundly affect some of the most vulnerable and frustrating clients. At the very least, readers may see a wider range of possibilities for complex clients. Instead of declaring, "The client is unwilling; suffers from character defects or has an Axis II disorder and character pathology," readers may understand that trauma can mimic, stimulate, or cause a wide range of changes. This book will stimulate a different way of seeing today's complex clients, those who suffer from blends of disorders that are often linked together by traumatic circumstances.

So, what do we know and not know about the effects of trauma? How is trauma related to addiction? What about the role of genetics? Can trauma be an excuse? Do events cause addiction or just lead to increased drinking? Do I treat traumatized clients differently from addicts? Can addiction cause a trauma-related condition? Which do we treat first? What is known about trauma-related disorders? Is biology affected or just perception? Can we cure this condition? What techniques work? What about moral responsibility? Why do some of these clients seem bent on self-destruction? How do I talk to clients with co-occurring phenomena? Why do they seem so angry? How do I tell them the truth without causing them further injury? What exactly is post-traumatic stress disorder (PTSD) and how is it treated? How are the Steps connected to this?

The following chapters will help answer some of these questions. Indeed, we are dealing with more complex clients. Do not be intimidated by the differences in clinical terminology. This is all about language and understanding. What at first may look like a cacophony of issues will hopefully become simpler as the reader progresses from the foundations to clinical application. As has been observed in a completely different field, theoretical physics, "At the convergence of complexity and chaos lies simplicity." The reader will develop a deeper understanding and more accurate perception of what these compelling clients need in order to identify and deal better with the convergence of addiction and trauma-based disorders.

Confusion is common, but complexity can yield to simplicity.

■ ■ ■

CHAPTER ONE

THE BASICS OF POST-TRAUMATIC STRESS DISORDER

The clients of today are more complicated than those of twenty-five years ago. In addition to treating clients with addictions, today's clinicians and counselors are dealing with clients who also have multiple psychiatric diagnoses. If you ask addiction counselors, "When is the last time you saw a straightforward, simple alcoholic?" most will politely chuckle. It seems that the level of client difficulty and complexity grows every year.

It is no coincidence that the term "co-occurring disorders" has entered our daily vocabulary. Perhaps this is the result of being trained to look for more, but I think that explanation is too simple. It is my supposition that the clients we treat today are in fact more complex than those we treated twenty-five years ago. Why, is not clear. Part of the answer may be a change in our environment, culture, and experiences.

Understanding the basic mechanisms of stress and trauma may help us understand this complexity, which individuals are most vulnerable, and how they are impacted. By reviewing the basics, we can glean more than a few clinical insights.

Can Trauma Disorders Account for Part of the Surge in Co-occurring Disorders?

This is a deceptively complex question, and I will not bore the reader with the theoretical debates. I will state, however, that trauma-related disorders may play a substantial role in the increased number of clients with an addiction and a psychiatric disorder. Modern illicit drugs are far more potent and toxic. For example, marijuana today is not the same as the less powerful variants of the 1960s. Young people today are exposed to an array of powerful substances whose long-term effects have yet to be discerned. Addicts are also exposed to traumatic consequences at an earlier age. Many of today's club drugs assault brain chemistry and emotional integrity. Young people are exposed to more toxins that may trigger specific psychiatric conditions. How much of this exposure is chemical and how much is emotional is part of the debate. However, young people are having harsher psychological consequences at an earlier age. Whereas alcohol has always been associated with physical assault and sexual assault, today's club drug combinations increase the likelihood of rape and at an earlier age than a generation ago. The consequences are devastating and may set off powerful reactions.

Traumatic reactions, both emotional and physical, are possibly part of the reason addicts today are so much harder to understand and treat. We do know that trauma results in a wide range of symptoms setting off depression, dissociation, anxiety, phobias, and interpersonal changes. Trauma may be the key variable in the so-called Axis II disorders. The bottom line is that science will sort out this puzzle, but many clinicians with expertise in trauma disorders, including myself, believe that reactions to trauma can explain many psychological conditions. I also believe that exposure to trauma greatly increases the likelihood of developing an addiction.

Addiction increases the likelihood of trauma-related disorders, and trauma-related disorders increase the probability of addiction. This is part of the reason that it is vital that today's clinicians understand both addiction and trauma-related disorders. The blend of these two conditions in clients results in a need for more sophisticated clinical services. The more we understand the basics of both disciplines, the more able we are to help clients who don't seem to be getting better with techniques that seemed to work well decades ago.

Trauma and the Numbers

Estimates vary but the *lifetime* rate (essentially how many of us over a lifespan are likely to develop this disorder) of post-traumatic stress disorder (PTSD) is about 10 to 12 percent. (Some samples place the rate at 8 to 10 percent, and this may reflect sample error or difference in criteria or instrumentation.) Therefore, about one in ten people will collide with unmanageable circumstances that will ultimately result in traumatic symptoms that meet current criteria for a diagnosis of PTSD. It should also be noted that many clinicians think the diagnostic criteria is too demanding and should be "loosened up." Others believe the exact opposite. Some still wish to get rid of the PTSD diagnosis.

Gender affects the rate of PTSD occurrence in the United States. The *life-time* prevalence for females is estimated at 10 to 15 percent, whereas the life-time estimate for males is about 5 to 8 percent, again varying with the sample and researcher. The gender difference may be a reflection in symptom manifes-tation, not resistance to pathology. The lower incidence for males possibly re-sults from the fact that many males, particularly young males, act out rather than act in. As such, many males display disorders that might be diagnosed as impulsiveness, intermittent explosive disorder, or sociopathy instead of PTSD. Males with PTSD also appear to have higher rates of attention deficit disorder (ADD) and attention-deficit hyperactivity disorder (ADHD). Which came first (the ADD/ADHD or the PTSD) is not entirely clear.

The above estimates were derived prior to the bombing of the World Trade Center on September 11, 2001, reflecting an affluent society at peace. This suggests that even in an amazingly affluent and peaceful culture, people are still exposed to traumatic events.

Originally, only combat veterans were studied and diagnosed with PTSD. As we move ahead in time, more and more groups are subsequently included under the PTSD rubric. These people include victims of domestic violence, rape, incest, and automobile accidents; parents of SIDS (sudden infant death syndrome) children and parents with children on transplant lists; individuals diagnosed with a fatal illness; victims of street crimes; and children taunted at school. It would appear that exposure to toxic or overwhelming events is more the norm today than the exception.

Now, what about PTSD's connection to addiction? We now know that people with active PTSD have a much higher probability of substance abuse or dependence than the average population. It would appear that the correlation is about .80. Thus, about 64 percent of those individuals with an active case of PTSD will also have a substance abuse problem, and perhaps a full-blown addictive disorder. This rate is actually lower than the connection observed in other populations, including the veteran population. Some veteran studies re-port a correlation as high as .90, but this varies with different samples. Cer-tainly any clinician working with combat-related PTSD encounters significant levels of addiction and severe abuse.

So, what is the likelihood that a client in an addiction treatment program has PTSD? The estimates range from 10 to 50 percent, depending upon whom and when you ask. Twenty years ago, we might have believed that clients were only addicts (they did not also have PTSD or other mental illnesses). More recently, we have discovered this is not true. Whether this is just an increase in awareness or a change of a more fundamental nature is debatable. In my opinion, we are seeing *both*. Thus, in the average treatment program, we would likely find about 33 percent of the clients in treatment for an addictive disorder also have PTSD. I suspect that this is about the rate we would also find in Alcoholics Anonymous (AA) or Narcotics Anonymous (NA) meetings.

What percentage of individuals exposed to traumatic events, including rape, street crimes, automobile accidents, and war, develop PTSD? The answer seems to be about 25 percent. Why do some develop this condition upon exposure and others do not? What happens to the other 75 percent? These questions are being actively explored, researched, and debated.

It would appear that social support systems, religious/spiritual beliefs, and genetic factors play a role. There is also a connection to expectation, training, context of exposure, and leadership. One of the earliest observations about "emotional breakdown" during combat is that units with good leadership had lower psychiatric casualty rates. Those with accurate expectations and good training also seem to be "spared." Actual training programs are geared toward "stress inoculation." We can train people to be more resistant to stress-related symptom development. Perhaps the most efficient stress inoculation training system we have is the U.S. military. Basic training and specialty combat training teach individuals to function in the face of chaos and to follow orders, not impulse. We need to remember, however, that we can train soldiers and other groups to suppress feelings, but many will become symptomatic over the course of time.

PTSD was only one of several names considered for post-traumatic phenomena. "Delayed stress" was also a contender because exposure to an event may not result in symptoms for months, years, or even decades after the event. Many World War II veterans functioned without symptoms until they hit retirement years, had fewer distractions, or viewed thematic movies like *Saving Private Ryan*. This time lapse is part of what makes our estimates confusing. For example, the average incest survivor will not display symptoms until he or she is about thirty years of age. Thus, 25 percent as our population norm for exposure to symptom development may be a low estimate in part because the survivors may not have been studied for a long enough time period.

Types of Traumatic Events

The rate of symptom development depends upon the nature of the traumatic event. If we first look at acts of nature, such as earthquakes, tornadoes, or hurricanes, the general connection between the event and symptom development is lower than the global 25 percent rate. Although we get considerable variation from sample to sample, it would appear that an act of God produces PTSD only 4 to 15 percent of the time (some findings are higher, depending upon content and sample).

However, for events connected to human-to-human boundary violations or violence, the percentage of people who develop symptoms rises to about 80 percent (the range tends to be 60 percent to 90 percent, depending upon the sample). If we track victims of rape, the connection appears to be 80 percent. Similar findings are reported for victims of street crimes. Prostitutes also have an 80 percent rate of PTSD.

In addition to showing the relationship between PTSD and the different types of traumatic events, table 1 summarizes the general prevalence of PTSD, the relationship between PTSD and addiction, as well as the percentage of addicts likely to be suffering from PTSD.

TABLE 1: POST-TRAUMATIC STRESS DISORDER BASIC NUMBERS	
Incidence of PTSD in the general population	10 to 12 percent
Correlation of active PTSD and addiction	R = .80
Addicts in primary treatment with PTSD	33 percent (10 to 50 percent)
Incidence of PTSD following a traumatic event	25 percent
Incidence of PTSD following a natural disaster	4 percent (4 to 15 percent)
Incidence of PTSD following a man-made disaster	80 percent (60 to 90 percent)

It would appear that acts of man are far more likely to result in confusion, blame, anger, repressed anger, self-loathing, obsessional thinking, and overt PTSD than acts of God. Attribution appears to play a vital role. Clients are more likely to let go of blame if they see no intended malice or if they recognize they have no control over the outcome. Conversely, clients are more likely to take responsibility or feel they should have control when person-to-person violations occur.

Stress 101: The Basics

In order to appreciate how trauma affects ordinary people, we must first consider what we know about stress in general. Once we understand the foundation we can begin to think about environment, genetics, and the powerful aftermath of trauma.

A Fundamental Law

Too little stress results in poor performance. Too much stress also results in poor performance. A moderate amount of stress produces peak performance, sometimes called the optimal level of performance. This is illustrated in figure 1 and it is called the Yerkes-Dodson law. Examine figure 1 carefully.

Figure 1 clearly shows us that we need some stress in order to perform well. Too little stress is unhealthy, as is too much. This relationship applies across all sorts of stress or anxiety situations, as well as all types of tasks, including emotional, cognitive, and athletic tasks. Originally derived from drive theory, the connection between stress and performance is so strong, it is one of the

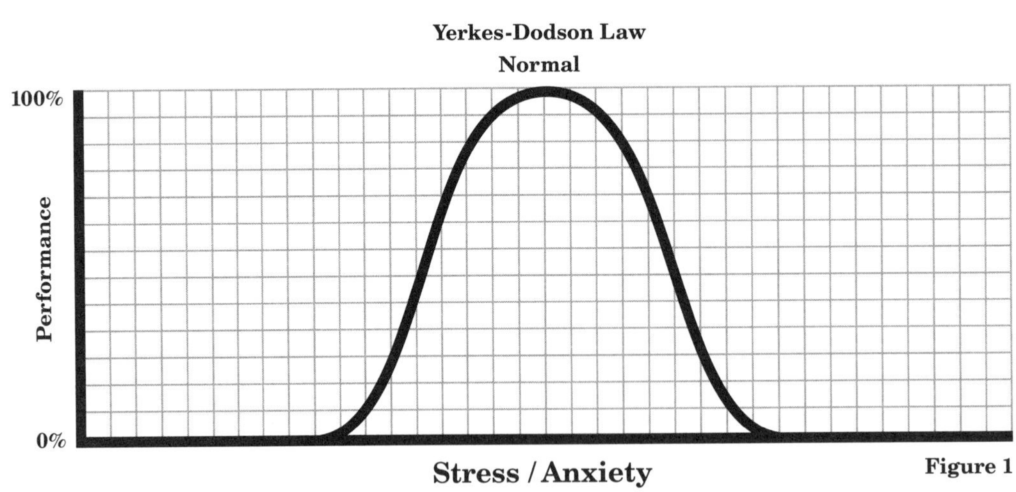

Figure 1

few psychological principles to be called a "law." It is a simple relationship, powerful and important.

Genetics

Nature plays a role in human behavior. In fact, it plays a large role. As you will note in figure 2, some people appear to be much more sensitive to stress.

If you look carefully at figure 2, you will note that the optimal level of stress arousal is a lot lower for this "sensitive" group of people. These individuals tend to function best at levels most of us would consider "boring." They tend to get overwhelmed with stress levels most of us would consider normal. They go through daily life with more anxiety than most. In fact, we would say this cluster of individuals is afflicted with "anxiety disorders." The most extreme manifestations of this cluster would result in full-blown phobias, including agoraphobia.

Classic anxiety disorders do seem to have a genetic link; they tend to run in family lines. It is also interesting to note that the favorite substances of choice for this group, which also has a high incidence of addictive disorders, are anxiolytics (addictive medication that lowers anxiety levels) and alcohol (which also has some anxiety-reducing features, at least upon initial ingestion).

Anxiety disorders are highly responsive to treatment. These individuals tend to respond well to behavioral interventions, systematic desensitization, relaxation training, guided imagery, exposure techniques, and cognitive-behavioral interventions. Some tend to respond favorably to selective serotonin reuptake inhibitors (SSRIs), whereas others are good candidates for antihypertensives along with behavioral techniques.

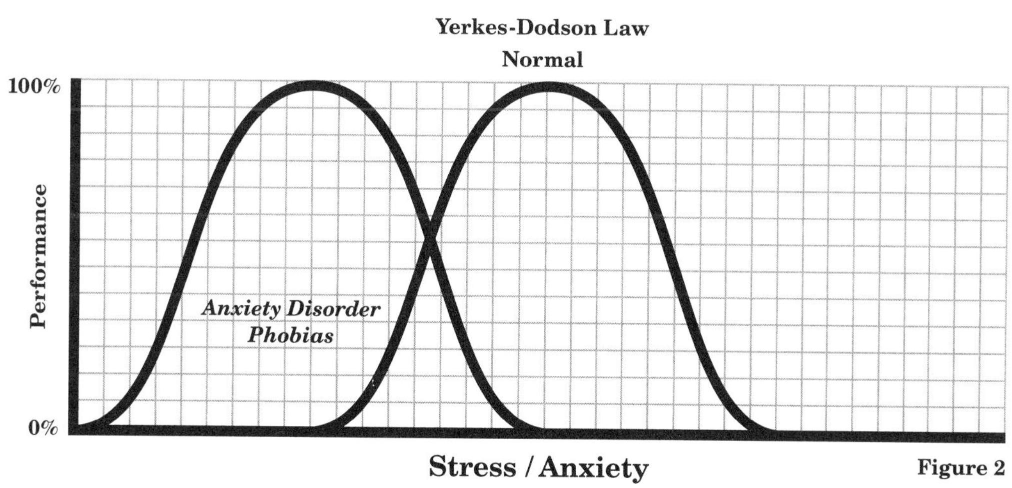

Figure 2

Hyper-responsivity to stress can be a gift. Individuals with heightened sensitivity tend to be artists and musicians. They see or hear things in ways the average person does not process. They also tend to have difficulty filtering out ancillary noise. Stimuli benign to the average person can be disruptive or disturbing.

We need to consider a genetic vulnerability before we jump to conclusions when performing our clinical duties. For example, I was treating a very bright, artistically gifted young woman with multiple problems, including suspected incest. At the time, we were dealing with some sensitive themes. When she came in for her next session, she mentioned that she had gone to the nearby art museum for the first time. She stated that when entering the museum, she began to cry. "Why?" I innocently asked. I suspected that she saw an art piece that triggered some uncomfortable thoughts or memories, and I was just waiting for the breakthrough connection. Her response to my inquiry was, "Doesn't everybody cry when they see all those magnificent colors?" She reported that this had happened to her all her life, and she indicated that many of her artist friends did the same thing. She was puzzled when, in response to her direct inquiry, I told her that was not my experience. In fact, since my wiring is average, I tend to think about how long I am going to look at a picture, where the gift shop is, and do they have a coffee shop or cafeteria. Yes, beauty and art are in the eye of the beholder, and genetic levels of sensitivity may be a partial factor.

On the opposite end of the spectrum (see figure 3), there are individuals whose inherent responsivity to stress is a *higher* threshold of arousal. That is, it takes more stress for these individuals to reach their optimal level of arousal.

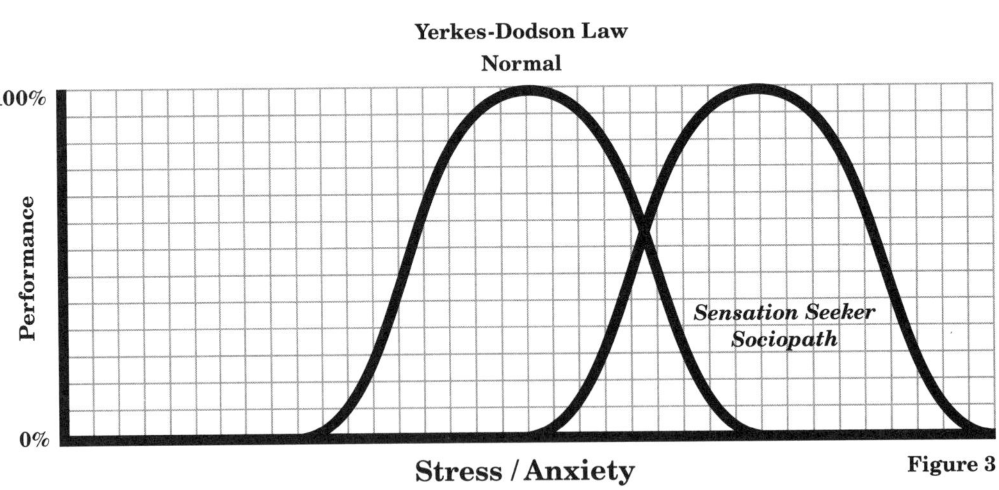

Figure 3

These individuals tend to be bored under circumstances that the average person would call optimally challenging. They find the typical challenges of life "boring." They do not find stimulation, meaning, or arousal when facing typical life challenges. They do not feel pressure to perform in school or work perceived as boring. Alternatively, they perform with peak efficiency under conditions most of us would call stressful. They tend to choose careers and hobbies that involve risk, excitement, and above-average levels of challenge. We would refer to these individuals as "sensation seekers." There is considerable evidence to suggest a genetic link. Members of the medical profession tend to belong to this group, as do individuals in the mental health and addictions treatment profession. Some of us are here due to sensation seeking, or as Irvin Yalom (2000) has noted, a proclivity toward voyeurism, while others are here as a result of exposure to addiction or trauma.

Extreme sensation seekers might become sociopaths, particularly if they see the "system" as the main challenge. A more adaptive variant would be someone who chooses pro-social, high-risk endeavors. Entrepreneurs, for example, tend to be risk-takers and sensation seekers. In addition to members of the medical community, individuals who join the military, firefighters, and law enforcement personnel tend toward this "circuitry." A more ambiguous position would be that of politician or CEO, some of whom are pro-social, and all too many of whom are sociopaths. As with a genetic loading for anxiety, being wired for sensation seeking is not inherently good or bad. How this energy is channeled, managed, and directed matters.

Environment

We know that genetics are powerful, but in any given discussion of behavior, environment accounts for anywhere from 40 to 60 percent of the variance. So, for the sake of our examination, assume that the majority of people start off with an average stress response pattern. Examine figure 4 closely.

The middle curve represents how the average person responds to stress. The curves to the right and left represent the shift in performance we would expect to see as the result of exposure to an overwhelming stressor. In this scenario, the average individual is transformed by the stress exposure and may act like those people represented in the curve to the right, or he or she may shift to the other extreme and perform like those represented in the curve to the left.

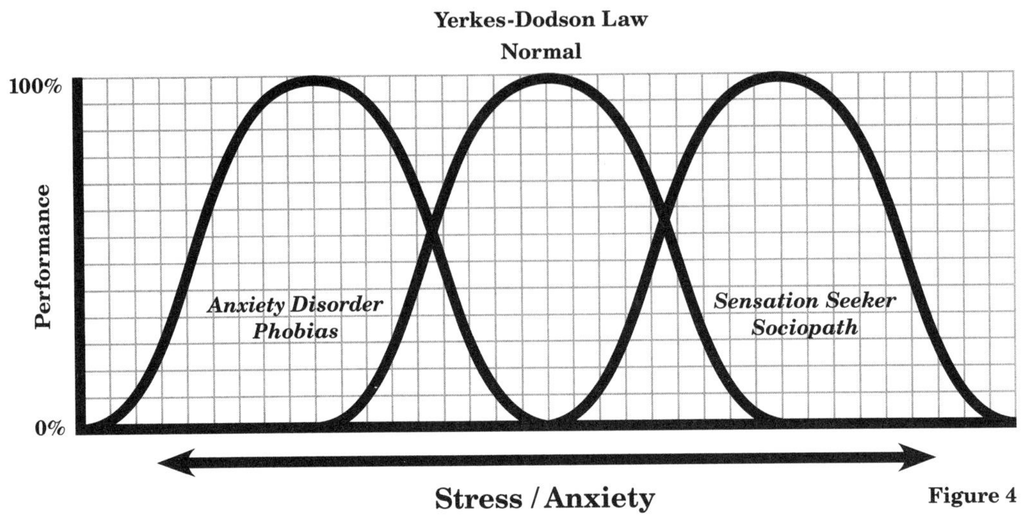

Figure 4

The question becomes: What happens to the average individual when he or she is exposed to unmanageable, fear-inducing, and perhaps life-threatening levels of stress? Do these individuals gravitate toward heightened sensitivity (anxiety disorders) or toward sensation seeking? Professionals and clients alike often fail to answer this question correctly. The answer is *both.* Exposure to an extreme stressor tends to create a vacillating pattern where we observe *both* anxiety disorders and sensation seeking. In clinical terms, we see post-traumatic phenomena as resulting in an anxiety disorder and/or dissociation. Dissociation infers a lack of emotional connectedness and is very often associated with high-risk-taking behavior. In fact, there was considerable debate during the preparation of the third edition of the *Diagnostic and Statistical Manual of Mental Disorders (DSM-III)* as to whether PTSD should be categorized as an anxiety disorder or a dissociative disorder. Once again, the correct answer should be both. However, a decision was made to place PTSD under the rubric of anxiety disorders where it has remained ever since.

People exposed to trauma go through a transformation. They become more anxious, and/or they become sensation seekers. The most common pattern is for periodic vacillation in terms of style. A sexually anorexic rape survivor may suddenly swing toward aggressive acting-out or sensation seeking. The cycle that included seductive behavior or overt acting-out contributed to our tradition of blaming the victim.

This contradictory phenomenon is a key to understanding the emotional aftermath of trauma. On the one hand, the survivors are frightened to death.

On the other hand, they are so inured that they no longer care. Consciously or unconsciously as a function of dissociation, these individuals engage in acting-out or sensation seeking.

This contradiction in behavioral patterns is one of the key markers of PTSD. It most often cycles between extremes, but on occasion we observe simultaneity. The following case study is a classic illustration of this simultaneity.

CASE STUDY: SAL

Sal, an articulate, short, stocky, and powerfully built man, was referred by his Employee Assistance Program for treatment of acrophobia, a fear of heights. Sal felt very uncomfortable going above the third floor in any building. (Fortunately my office at the time was on the third floor, his upper comfort limit, although the glass elevator added to his distress.) Sal sought assistance because his job as a construction supervisor required that he climb to the top of the then relatively new microwave towers that were appearing all over the city. Sal was visibly distressed by the prospect of climbing these towers and indicated that this issue was what he wanted to work on.

Before formulating a treatment strategy, I decided that I needed more information. Sal proceeded to inform me that he was an alcoholic, clean and sober six years. Sal had a sponsor, sponsored others, and was deeply involved in a Twelve Step program of recovery. I asked Sal several more questions and learned that he was passionate about recovery. In fact, he was so passionate that he felt he needed to contribute to the community. Sal lived in a blue-collar suburb adjacent to a poor community that drug dealers had infiltrated. Sal was frustrated. Sal's numerous calls to the police did not change the situation. So, Sal decided he needed to act on his own. He planned on going to the main thoroughfare after work and confronting the crack dealers. He calmly told me that he had a gun tucked under his jacket. He had flashed it recently during one highly charged verbal exchange. The police had been called and Sal was almost arrested (fortunately he had a permit for the weapon).

> So, here we have an intelligent, rational, and sensitive man, with good reality testing, who was displaying completely contradictory behaviors. How could someone afraid of an elevator (where the likelihood of injury is far less than a lightning strike) be fearless while trying to intimidate a crack dealer? Before you read the rest of the story, try to envision how this contradiction might have occurred. Assume—and this is an accurate assumption—that this man is bright, rational, and did not have a preexisting mental illness. How could he be dangerously confrontational and terrified of heights at the same time? Not logical until you know his history.
>
> Sal served as a helicopter crew chief during his two tours of duty in Vietnam. He was involved in three helicopter crashes, two of which he was the sole survivor. Sal was intensely patriotic, yet distrustful of the systems that let him down. He felt that it was imperative to protect one's family and community. If the system wasn't going to do it, he would have to take action on his own. Risk of injury protecting loved ones was not an issue. Heights and feelings of helplessness was another story.

This case clearly illustrates the possibility of simultaneity: You can be terrified and heroic or dissociative at the same time. We are dealing with opposites that are not mutually exclusive. When you feel these contradictory urges, the tendency is to declare yourself crazy, as was the case with Sal. Sal succeeded in therapy, mastering his fear of heights. Some simple behavioral imaging techniques were remarkably effective, as was our review of his helplessness, guilt, and fear surrounding the three tragic crashes. It is interesting that Sal transcended the fear but not the anger. He gave up his gun and let go of the need to clean up the streets in vigilante fashion. However, he became more and more distrustful of his immediate supervisor, who played some corporate games and was less than totally truthful. Many survivors have absolutely no tolerance for dishonesty or duplicity in others, even if they themselves indulge in the same behavior during their addiction or an episode of emotional regression. Survivors strive for justice and honesty, and have a hard time with ambiguity and disingenuous behaviors. Sal got into a verbal altercation with his boss and decided to resign after making some threats against this man's life.

Sal is now happily retired and justifiably receives disability from the Veterans Administration (VA) for his PTSD. He lives with his wife in rural New England and continues to help others with their recovery. He no longer engages in confrontation and cherishes his recovery and serenity.

In most instances of PTSD, we see vacillation between extremes and occasionally simultaneity. Survivors tend to feel "split apart" after their trauma. They secretly feel crazy, damaged, and contradictory. They do not realize that this phenomenon is completely normal and predictable. Freudian clinicians have referred to this as "ego-splitting" or "ego fractionation." It is nothing mystical or unusual; it is just what happens to normal people following a toxic, traumatic episode.

Traumatic events have a definite connection to addiction. Trauma-related disorders may be part of the surge in co-occurring disorders. Exposure to traumatic events may or may not produce symptoms, and different types of events appear to play a role. Traumatic natural events are not as likely to produce disturbance as are person-to-person violations. Clients who develop PTSD suffer from a set of contradictory symptoms that affect attitude, behavior, biology, and self-perception. These symptoms may be part of what we are challenged with when treating today's clients of increased complexity.

■ ■ ■

CHAPTER TWO

DEFINITIONS AND DIAGNOSIS OF PTSD

The goal of this chapter is to provide clinicians with a set of working definitions of PTSD. These definitions will help clinicians understand the range and depth of trauma-related disorders and shape clinical attitudes, styles, and interventions. Teach these definitions to your clients.

We will begin with the most basic and empowering definition, one that all clients and clinicians should integrate into their clinical thinking. Subsequent definitions become more complex, but they describe, in brief sentences, PTSD at a deeper level. All of the definitions consider factors that help clinicians understand why some people develop the disorder and other people do not. The final definition moves us into complex post-traumatic stress disorder (complex PTSD or CPTSD). Knowing what CPTSD is can help clinicians avoid a common, invalidating diagnostic error.

Subsequent to the working definitions, we'll review the fourth edition of the *Diagnostic and Statistical Manual of Mental Disorders (DSM-IV-TR)* criteria for PTSD. The juxtaposition of helplessness and anger will be explored, as well as the question of how much impact an individual has on controlling events, as well as the issue of trauma in mood disorders and character pathology. Moving beyond the *DSM-IV-TR*, the connection between PTSD and dissociative identity disorder (DID), previously known as multiple personality disorder (MPD), will be reviewed, as well as factitious disorders. Finally, methods of diagnosis, including some specific tools, as well as the art form of diagnosis, will be discussed.

What Is Post-traumatic Stress Disorder?

In this section, we will explore five definitions I have derived and utilized over the years. The first definition is simple. Subsequent definitions provide a foundation for clinician and client to begin understanding what this condition really is.

Definition 1: PTSD Is a Normal Response to Abnormal Events

This is perhaps the most vital and empowering declaration clinicians can provide traumatized clients. This definition is as fundamental to trauma-based disorders as the disease concept is to alcoholism. Surprisingly, many clients given a formal diagnosis of PTSD do not hear or understand this fundamental definition, which defines the event(s), not the person, as abnormal. Perceiving PTSD as a normal response to an abnormal event shifts responsibility, perceived control, and, most important, guilt. Clients are reminded that they were normal before the event and that these reactions, which not everyone develops, follow a fairly universal pattern.

In the first chapter, we learned that powerful events can cause individuals to become fearful and disconnected (dissociative) all at once. They become insensitive, yet hypersensitive, and their egos are torn asunder. They tend to act in an illogical, inconsistent manner, often combining anger and guilt. Serene, rational people, following exposure to powerful events, can be transformed. There is nothing mystical about this process. It can happen to anyone, just ask a combat veteran or a rape survivor. Clients can feel out of control; their behaviors are contradictory and illogical; and they tend to make decisions based on impulse. These clients are confused and feel insane. Most of us have had similar episodes following a tragic loss or traumatic event. We feel numb, disconnected, "out of it," hypersensitive, and highly emotional. However, it is the persistent nature of a fairly universal stress reaction that differentiates acute distress from the clinical syndrome.

Researchers continue to struggle with the factors that increase or decrease the risk of developing PTSD. We cannot yet identify an "invisible line," but known factors appear to affect the likelihood of onset. These factors are called *moderator variables.* They include support systems, age, and the frequency, intensity, and duration of an event.

As a clinically driven statement, our first definition is unequivocally valid. It helps the clinician normalize clients' feelings and permits new thinking about guilt and shame. Survivors tend to feel completely responsible for the unmanageable. This is a core component of immediate and long-term shame-based thinking that is the bedrock of psychopathology.

Some may claim that defining PTSD as a normal reaction to an abnormal situation removes personal responsibility. This concern is valid. There are negligent, angry, and intoxicated people with PTSD who hurt others. Sometimes there is a fine line between perpetrator and victim, as well as confusion between explanation and excuse. As client advocates, we need to be very careful here. We do not wish to give clients a "free ticket" or "abuse excuse." Though we advocate responsible behavior, we must try to lessen the internal chorus of self-blame.

One of our roles as clinicians is to provide implicit or explicit relief from guilt. Shell shock victims during World War I taught us that survivor guilt was a huge factor in the development of symptomatology. Clients tended to get better when they learned to accept they could not control uncontrollable events. Forgiveness by clinicians starts a process toward self-forgiveness. The need for relief from guilt has not changed among trauma survivors.

The *DSM-IV-TR* does not clearly articulate this simple, forgiveness-oriented definition. Our first definition normalizes, shifts clients away from guilt and shame, and provides a first step in recovery. However, as we have learned with other disorders, including addiction, even valid and simple definitions do not stick readily.

Definition 2: PTSD Is a Chronic and Phasic Condition in Which Symptoms Are Multidimensional, Contradictory, and Highly Responsive to Treatment

As we move toward a more complex definition of PTSD, recognize that we are dealing with more than a transitory condition; it is a condition that produces confusion for client and clinician, affects more than one system, and is eminently treatable. In order to simplify, let's break this definition into components.

Chronic and Phasic

Most often, acute stress reactions diminish with time. According to the *DSM-IV-TR,* acute stress can last up to six months. However, if symptoms persist or develop after that time period, we call it post-traumatic stress disorder. One point of confusion is that post-traumatic stress can lie dormant for long periods. Acute symptoms may end, but they can return years or decades later. Sometimes people will not have stress reactions at the time of the event, but will become severely symptomatic well past the six-month time frame. Some individuals will have a long-delayed acute episode, and that is the end of it. However, when the stressors are of sufficient severity, we see long delays followed by recurrent symptom intrusion. For some survivors, like those of the Oklahoma City bombing on April 19, 1995, severe symptoms did not develop until they witnessed the World Trade Center disaster on September 11, 2001. In general, once a long delay occurs and a trauma-related disorder develops, it tends to come and go, almost as if some invisible threshold has been crossed. The condition becomes chronic and does not lend itself to simple "cures."

Once that invisible line is crossed, the client is likely to have this condition in some form during his or her lifespan. This condition is of critical importance for clinicians to understand. We cannot and should not purport to cure a condition that is so often chronic. Indeed, there are variations in the continuum. As we observe with addictive substances, some individuals may have several severe episodes without developing a full-blown addiction. Those who do become addicts need to accept the chronicity of their condition.

Similarly, many if not most clients who meet criteria for PTSD will have to deal with this condition throughout their lives. This is not to say that they will be disabled or dysfunctional. Indeed, the condition comes and goes, but it can get better with treatment. The phasic nature of PTSD can give the illusion that it is gone or in some instances never occurred. Once the clinician embraces the mercurial nature of PTSD, he or she is in a much better position to assist clients with this disorder.

Misunderstanding the chronicity and phasic nature of PTSD has led many to seek a cure. The expectation of a cure may be misleading. PTSD tends to come and go; this is the nature of the condition. Relapse or re-triggering of trauma symptoms is part of the fabric for most clients. As with addiction, our goal is not to cure, but to teach clients how to live with and manage the condition. Note that addicts who develop PTSD or survivors who develop an addiction tend to have more severe variants of both conditions.

Multidimensional

People who develop chronic symptoms in response to unmanageability and trauma are affected in all areas of functioning. This seemingly simple and intuitive conclusion seems to be absent from many treatment paradigms. Symptoms begin in one dimension—biological, cognitive, interpersonal, or spiritual—and later spread across all these spheres, rippling like a stone thrown into a pond. The bigger the stone, the farther out the waves spread.

PTSD is a "cunning and baffling" condition. As with an addictive disorder, all spheres of functioning are affected in clients with more severe consequences or symptoms. We observe obvious consequences in the interpersonal realm as relationships are severely disrupted, sometimes in very subtle ways. Survivors with PTSD tend to become isolated. Specific changes in biology and cognition, discussed in subsequent chapters, contribute to a lack of disclosure and connection with others.

Following a traumatic event(s), it is normal to feel disconnected from others. Long ago, clinicians described this process, called dissociation, as "disconnecting" from one's body. Clients tend to describe acute dissociation as a shift in perception. In fact, it is almost by description a dimensional shift. Many individuals report that when they feel stressed or intensely afraid, they "rise above their bodies." We are not talking about astral projection, but a biologically driven shift that permits us to endure pain. One no longer sees the world in three dimensions. With a fear-based reality, you suddenly see the world in two dimensions. If you imagine looking at your hands, it is as if they move far away from you, are not part of your body, and seem detached, in two- rather than three-dimensional space.

If you have never experienced intense fear, this may sound psychotic. However, it is not. It is simply a normal reaction to a fear-based situation: All senses are affected, the heart races, hormones shift, and your dimensional perspective, and to some extent your anchoring in a three-dimensional reality, is affected. Most people return to reality quickly, and the episode ends. Those who develop PTSD don't return to their bodies and they no longer feel normal. They no longer dwell in three-dimensional space. As a result, they no longer feel connected to those around them, including (and sometimes particularly) loved ones.

Changes in cognition are almost self-evident. Survivors speak differently to themselves, often repeating shame-based messages. "Cognitive intrusions" disrupt thought processes; memories flood the senses and overwhelm thought. These intrusions can be multisensory, involving auditory, tactile, and visual intrusion. It is as if the "channel" has been suddenly changed, disrupting reality testing for seconds, sometimes longer, but often leaving a lingering shift in cognitive focus and thought patterns.

Dissociation is definitely a real phenomenon and perhaps one of the most effective natural tools we have to protect ourselves from actual danger.

Dissociation occurs on a daily basis, even without pain. We learn to split off pieces of our reality in everyday life. If you drive a car, listen to the radio, and talk on a cell phone all at the same time, you are dissociating. Dissociation, like so many conditions, is part of a continuum. In my opinion, the more severe form of dissociation is not a separate disorder, as listed in the *DSM-IV-TR* under dissociative identity disorder (DID), once called multiple personality disorder (MPD). DID and PTSD are simply part of the continuum of dissociation. As mentioned in the previous chapter, when compiling the classifications for the *DSM-III,* clinicians debated whether to categorize PTSD as an anxiety disorder or as a dissociative disorder, and decided on the former. In reality, trauma-based disorders belong, I believe, in both categories. Simply stated, lesser forms of PTSD are anxiety based, whereas the more severe forms (CPTSD and borderline personality disorder) are dissociation based.

If you are confused, do not worry. The vocabulary is daunting. However, I find it remarkably simple to think of trauma-based disorders (PTSD and CPTSD) as part of a continuum of disorders that includes anxiety, dissociation, and such arcane diagnoses as borderline personality disorder and DID. Trauma disorders include a full range of anxiety and dissociation. All of these, by definition, are normal reactions to unmanageable or painful events.

Biological shifts in the wake of severe stress are rather profound. Entire biological systems get triggered, involving several pathways of change, affecting the sympathetic and parasympathetic systems, and specific areas of the brain, particularly the amygdala. These changes will be explained in the next chapter.

Survivors who become symptomatic tend to go through profound changes in their spiritual systems. Some drop out of religious participation altogether, but the majority change in more subtle ways. Whereas they ultimately blame themselves for what went wrong, they also become angry with their Higher Power, God, or religion. The more symptomatic an individual becomes, the more severe the spiritual disturbance. Almost all clients with the PTSD diagnosis develop "a foreshortened sense of future," a symptom that is common to all anxiety-based disorders. Most clinicians think of this in terms of cognitive disruption, but I tend to see it as a spiritual crisis. Clients no longer have faith that things will work out for them. They may say, "Everything went wrong that day [the day of the trauma], and since then, everything has been screwed up. I'll never be happy again, and I will never feel safe or trust others. I don't see God as a loving protector. I feel abandoned and hopeless." In general, the more severe the trauma, the more likely we will witness a severe spiritual disruption. The most severe disruptions tend to result in nihilism—the complete loss of faith in all belief systems, meaning, purpose, or destiny.

Contradictory

Individuals who have PTSD display many contradictory features. They are overwhelmed with fear, yet engage in sensation seeking. Sexual abuse survivors tend to become sexually anorexic, but then have episodes or phases of hypersexuality. They are terrified of intimacy and crave intimacy. They wish to be touched, but demand nobody come near them. They are idealistic, yet incredibly cynical. They have profound sensitivity, yet they can be completely insensitive. They are fear based, but highly impulsive. They can be paranoid, then reckless. They are kind, but they are capable of being vicious. They think too much, but behave impulsively. They experience cognitive intrusion, but they are highly avoidant. They think about events and anniversaries, yet they avoid rituals or anniversaries.

If you examine the definitions and symptoms of PTSD in the *DSM-IV-TR,* the first cluster of symptoms is essentially the antithesis of the second cluster of symptoms. Cluster one revolves around cognitive intrusion, flashbacks, obsessional thinking, emotional flooding, and feeling overwhelmed. Cluster two revolves around avoidance, cognitive and interpersonal. In general, we can expect individuals with this condition to display behaviors that are inconsistent and illogical to the outside observer. In general, the more severe the case, the more contradiction. Contradiction reflects and defines PTSD. Ignorance of this basic principle has fed the unfortunate tradition of judging, criticizing, and invalidating symptomatic survivors.

One manifestation of the contradiction in PTSD clients is the juxtaposition of arrogance and shame-based thinking. Clients with PTSD tend to experience classic shame-based thoughts and feelings. They believe that they caused the chaos or failed to control it. This belief, referred to as "magical thinking," often flies in the face of objective logic. For a classic example, imagine your combat buddy standing next to you. You ask him to walk over to a tree to pick up equipment you left there. Suddenly, you hear gunfire. Your buddy is spun around and ripped apart in front of your eyes. You think that you caused him to die. He went where you should have been and therefore you believe that you are at fault.

As a result of their experience, many PTSD clients believe they are unique. Such a client might say, "I can't talk to Joe since his worst trauma was getting a speeding ticket. Nobody has had it rougher than me. Nobody can understand." Thus, we have simultaneous shame and arrogance. The net result is isolation and silence.

Highly Responsive to Treatment

PTSD is a chronic condition, and a "cure" can be a psychonoxious expectation. However, PTSD is highly responsive to treatment. Many treatment approaches and options produce dramatic improvements. After treatment, clients may continue to get triggered, but not as easily. Triggers are less intrusive. Treatment, when applied to a sober client wanting help, can make a huge contribution toward recovery from both addiction and PTSD.

Definition 3: PTSD Is a Condition That Involves Affective Dysregulation

Judith Herman (1997) set forth this simple, yet powerful definition. Affective dysregulation simply means that the individual can no longer moderate or modulate emotion. He or she tends to respond to almost any subsequent situation with greater intensity than he or she would have prior to exposure to a trauma. At the time, Herman's definition was rather speculative. Thanks to amazing advances in brain-scanning technology, the data we have now dramatically demonstrates how accurate Herman's definition is.

Herman believes that exposure to events causes physical changes to the brain, making the management of emotional states, particularly those involving fear, much more difficult. Her notion is that cognition is no match for this intrusive, biologically driven process. No matter how rational the individual, when a triggering event occurs, emotions determine behavior. Herman believes that the limbic system essentially hijacks the person and overrides the higher executive and cortical function. Herman's definition accounts for some of the disparity between thought, intent, and actual behavior.

This sounds remarkably like the former director of the National Institute of Mental Health (NIMH) Dr. Stephen Hyman's description of addiction as "the hijacked brain." This neurological hijacking results in acting-out behaviors, sensation seeking, anger outbursts, and difficulty with interpersonal attachments. Anyone who has worked with survivors knows how emotionally driven they can be. Survivors tend to be moody, inconsistent, and resistant to rational interventions. Many suffer from formal depression. Others appear cyclothymic; that is, they have depression with euphoria but not quite mania.

Interestingly, several theories on relapse postulate a very similar process. One theory describes a neurobiological process that sets off a primitive urge when an addict is triggered. In this case, thought doesn't stand much of a chance. The limbic system, the more primitive portion of the brain (also known as the lizard brain), determines behavior. Again, higher cortical functions subsume control. Primitive urges become the basis for decision making and behavior.

What does this mean for the clinician? The dominance of the limbic system may be responsible for both relapse and trauma-related disorders. The primitive part of the brain overrides logic, intention, and declaration. Both PTSD and addiction appear to supercede predictable, logical decision making, and the culprit may be the primitive but powerful limbic system. In both conditions, we are not simply dealing with a lack of resolve.

Definition 4: PTSD Is a Disruption in the Flow of Consciousness

This is essentially the antithesis of Herman's definition, but has equal validity. Jerome Kroll (1993) describes PTSD as a condition that interrupts the normal flow of consciousness. If we define consciousness as that which is determined by higher cortical function, namely the neocortex, trauma and its aftermath cause a profound disruption in flow: Thinking is interrupted, and the brain goes "off-line." Kroll's description permits us to focus on the intrusive nature of PTSD wherein feelings and memories come forward with such force they disrupt the flow of thinking. Clients report feeling very distressed when this occurs. It is like having several radio or television stations playing simultaneously in their minds, making it difficult to track a single thought or pay attention to a conversation. Serenity and the normal internal set of images and internal processes are disrupted. A surge of raw feelings, disjointed images, flashbacks, and overwhelming noise replace the quiet voice in your head. The net result is that behavior, as with Herman's definition, is not based on higher executive function or baseline cognition. Trauma or traumatic triggers disrupt thinking and essentially displace your brain.

Again, this process is similar to Hyman's "hijacking" description. The main difference is that Kroll emphasizes the cognitive "noise" resulting from the splitting of consciousness that is part of dissociation. Dissociation, a remarkably effective defense, involves a splitting of consciousness, and some of the "noise" is not even processed at a conscious level. The person is "here, but not here."

Not surprisingly, we have opposite definitions of equal validity. Herman's definition fits with the biological override that robs the survivor of rational determinism. Kroll's definition describes an intrusive process that, in its fullest form, scrambles the flow of consciousness resulting in the essential opposite of serenity. Either definition encourages both clinician and survivor toward re-empowerment of rational function, or to put it more simply, reclaiming your higher brain. The real value in both of these definitions is that they reinforce a brain-based process wherein the survivor does not surrender control, but instead is overwhelmed or flooded by intrusive thoughts or a surging limbic system. These definitions can assist clients in understanding powerlessness. Surrender and powerlessness do not result in an abrogation of responsibility, but paradoxically provide clients with the freedom to make choices.

Definition 5: Complex Post-traumatic Stress Disorder and Borderline Phenomena Are Interchangeable

If we look at trauma as a continuum, the people who have more severe cases of PTSD have more severe and intrusive symptoms. These clients are more contradictory, confused, and difficult. They tend to be nihilistic and believe that nothing will ever be fair or right. They are moody, impossible to reason with, and very demanding.

Herman and others define the more severe form of PTSD as complex PTSD (CPTSD). Kroll articulately states that borderlines are simply clients with PTSD. He does not use Herman's distinction of CPTSD; however, Kroll simply declares that borderlines have PTSD and vice versa. Kroll was the first voice to set forth this notion, one that many clinicians had been thinking and quietly discussing.

Marsha Linehan (1993) also delineates a connection between trauma and borderline phenomena. Neither Kroll's declaration nor Linehan's observation made much of an impact at the time. Colin Ross's (2000) trauma model also made this powerful connection, again with little impact.

Perhaps there is confusion or even dissonance surrounding these conditions with identical symptoms and different traditions. If we examine the *DSM-IV-TR* definitions for PTSD and borderline personality disorder, we observe essentially identical symptoms, organized differently with some variations of emphasis.

One difference is the purported age of exposure or etiology. Borderline phenomenon is considered an early developmental problem. The term "borderline" has its foundation in the confused history of describing schizophrenia. It was thought that neurosis, an anxiety-based condition, was part of a continuum that with sufficient severity resulted in schizophrenic-like symptoms. The anxiety neurotic was the classic analytic client, and the interpretative framework was embraced at a literal level. More severe cases, those individuals who experienced early developmental trauma, developed symptoms that looked psychotic. The literature and clinical tradition surrounding borderline personality disorder developed *before* PTSD was recognized, defined, and accepted in the mental health world. Since borderline phenomena are so severe, it was listed as an Axis II or personality disorder. The main problem is that by definition, this condition is essentially untreatable. The label strikes fear in the hearts of clinicians and breeds hopelessness in clients carrying the diagnosis. Thus, defining complex PTSD as identical to borderline phenomena is a powerful reframing, one that fits the data, not arcane tradition. Borderlines are trauma survivors; they have the complex variant of PTSD; and indeed they are the most challenging, but highly treatable part of this continuum. In fact, it is probable that chronically relapsing clients, those resistant addicts who continue to fail in treatment, suffer from this co-occurring condition, complex PTSD, not borderline personality disorder.

Borderlines are part of the continuum of natural reactions to unmanageable events. Time of exposure and intensity of events both play a role in the development of CPTSD, too often referred to as hopeless borderlines. There is hope and these clients are eminently treatable.

As noted previously, one of the substantive differences in the two conditions is the emphasis on early childhood exposure. Fortunately, PTSD embraces this "difference." Early exposure is more potent than exposure later in life. The net result is not an untreatable condition, but simply complex PTSD. The differences from a theoretical perspective seem arbitrary and inconsequential. From a clinical perspective, the differences can be profound.

Research has also shown us that certain environmental factors provide protection from symptom development. These include social support systems and involvement in church or spiritual activities. Individuals with stronger social support systems seem to be able to "handle" more stress than those who are more thinly socialized. Similarly, a strong spiritual system, particularly if it includes activities and support of other members, can also provide invaluable protection. In addition, individuals fully engaged in projects, careers, community, or collective missions, particularly those that provide a sense of meaning, are equally well buffered.

DSM-IV–TR Criteria for PTSD Diagnosis

PTSD is in part a subjective phenomenon, more accurately a complex convergence of multiple genetic and moderator variables that determine pathology. The *DSM-III* required events (directly experienced or observed) outside the range of usual experience. The *DSM-IV-TR* wisely decided to remove the subjective measurement of event intensity. Exposure to a horrible event doesn't meet diagnostic criteria. We need an event(s) *and* symptoms. The list of possible event exposure has grown considerably over time. While we used to limit the criteria to war, rape, and incest, we now include other tragedies like car accidents and the death of a child. The *DSM-IV-TR* even includes receiving a diagnosis of a terminal illness.

In terms of some of the subtleties and underpinnings of the *DSM-IV-TR* diagnosis, normality is the inferred baseline prior to exposure. This is not always the case in the real world, but the philosophical underpinnings for PTSD do not assume a preexisting psychological condition. Freudian-based diagnoses prior to *DSM-III* assumed some developmental anomaly resulting in psychopathology. The inferential assumption of preexisting normality is revolutionary. The *assumption* of prior normality represents the civil equivalent of innocent unless proven guilty. Medical model tradition, at least in terms of mental health, was not always as generous.

You do not need to be physically injured in order to develop PTSD. In some cases, observing or bearing witness to trauma can result in PTSD. How do we know this?

Some of the earliest research involving airplane crashes showed that those involved in the aftermath, such as medics and paramedics, developed trauma symptoms of severity equal to those experienced by people involved in the crash. Actually, the earliest systematic studies of what we now call PTSD show that observers are affected. Survivors of railroad accidents in the 1840s developed a condition called railway spine thought to be purely physical. This condition also seemed to affect people who did not have a physical injury. Similarly, physicians treating shell shock, the syndrome identified in World War I, noticed many men became ill simply observing others being injured or killed. Vietnam veterans with physical wounds were *less* likely to develop PTSD than those without wounds or injury (assuming equivalent combat exposure). Some of the highest rates of PTSD were among medics, many of whom never fired a shot. Nurses and physicians, well behind the lines, were also at risk for developing this syndrome. Another high-risk group was the soldiers who prepared dead bodies for transport home. They may not have seen combat, but they certainly experienced its consequence. Observation can be as devastating as participation.

The "witness" factor also affects adult children of alcoholics. In some circles, this factor creates controversy. Not all adult children of alcoholics have enough chaos to generate PTSD. However, witness to family violence, particularly if repetitive and seen at an early age, can most certainly produce trauma-related disorders.

Another group of "witnesses" includes counselors and mental health professionals who are at risk of developing "secondary PTSD." Most clinicians fare well, but some are more vulnerable than others, since they themselves may have a history of having been traumatized. Many clinicians actually select a helping profession because of their own traumatic experiences and may meet personal needs providing therapy to others. A mixed blessing at times, this can be an asset as long as clinicians do not become so enmeshed as to lose grounding and become hardened or judgmental. Some clinicians lose sight of fundamental ethics and act out, thinking they are going to save their clients. Good self-maintenance is vital in clinical work. Clinical work is difficult and it can lead to cynicism, exhaustion, anger, or relapse. Early indicators include loss of empathy or the loss of the ability to hear clients with objectivity. Other indicators are acquiescing to every client intrusion, request, or demand, regardless of consequence and in defiance of standards of good practice. Be aware, seek peer support, and take action if you find yourself developing or redeveloping trauma-related conditions. Most clinicians rebound quickly, especially when they have the opportunity to articulate what they are dealing with.

Making the Diagnosis: Clinician Beware

If you are a counselor in an inpatient program, your main objective is identification, validation, treatment, and case management. It is imperative that PTSD be identified, but also be aware that PTSD is more likely to appear when you are looking for it. Obviously, there is some risk in overidentifying PTSD. The clinician can play into the hands of a malingerer, looking for an excuse, diversion, or manipulation. Indeed, some clients love to manipulate systems, attract attention, and tell mistruths for no apparent gain. Individuals who engage in this behavior may or may not be sociopaths. Another possibility is Munchausen syndrome and the whole class of conditions referred to as factitious disorders. The cause for factitious disorders is unknown, but some authors believe that perceived traumatic events may set off this condition. Many clinicians get angry with clients who have factitious disorders. Try not to judge the client on the basis of the event; what is traumatic to one individual is benign to another. Treating clinicians need to make a diagnostic differentiation, but that should not get in the way of maintaining empathy for clients whose symptoms are not clearly linked to identifiable traumatic events. Following is a case study that illustrates the difficulty of making a diagnosis.

CASE STUDY: MICHAEL

Michael, a small, powerfully built, tattooed, and confident-appearing Vietnam veteran, looked like a character from *American Graffiti.* He rode a loud motorcycle and slicked back his hair. He was a warm, friendly, uneducated, but very intelligent man who could crush you if he was angry. Michael was a combat-disabled veteran who displayed classic symptoms of PTSD. He spoke of vivid flashbacks, like slides in a movie projector, overtaking his consciousness. He would have fits of rage followed by profound anxiety often accompanied by staggering amounts of alcohol and pills. On one occasion, he had an armed standoff with the sheriff's office, believing that Vietcong regulars surrounded him. Michael was in and out of the hospital. Clearly unable to hold a job, he received 100 percent disability from the VA. He was a regular in outpatient and inpatient settings, and he took pride in helping teach interns about PTSD. A super raconteur, he was beloved by staff and fellow veterans.

Michael was a Special Forces soldier who told incredibly vivid war stories. He once described being held prisoner; another time

> he had his eyes blown out of their sockets. He spoke about more and more amazing situations, so amazing that some of his peers questioned his honesty. One veteran obtained Michael's military record, his DD-214, and his military hospital records. What he learned was that Michael was indeed a Special Forces Vietnam combat veteran, but his only wound was a self-inflicted gunshot wound to the leg. This truth circulated quickly in the veteran community. Staff loyal to Michael refused to accept it, regardless of documentation. Michael was never confronted directly, but he knew that something had changed. Hardened combatants, among others, considered Michael to be a fraud. Many clinicians now saw him as a person with a classic factitious disorder. His drinking escalated and so did his angry outbursts. Three years later Michael shot himself again, this time in the head during another drunken rage. So, was Michael a terminal alcoholic, constitutionally unable to get better, a factitious PTSD case, or a controversial casualty of a war with an unsettling history? The answer may depend upon your philosophy or politics.

Diagnosing PTSD can be trickier than one might suppose. Clients engage in denial and minimization, as they do with addictive substances. Some clients forget parts of their past. Identifying or failing to identify a traumatic event or series of events does not ensure a diagnosis of PTSD. Many conditions overlap PTSD, including anxiety disorders, depression, and bipolar disorders to name a few. In addition, clinician bias can enter the equation.

Fortunately, many diagnostic instruments can be of great value to the practicing clinician. The tools range from structured interviews to a series of true/false questions. Most of the instruments are quickly administered, and some, such as the Trauma Symptom Inventory, give actual scores that include validity scales. The National Center for Post-traumatic Stress Disorder provides a comprehensive list of the assessment tools available to clinicians. For some invaluable resources, please refer to www.ncptsd.org/publications/assessment/.

Many clinicians avoid formal tools in assessing PTSD, due to limitations in time, resources, or training in formal psychological testing. Some highly experienced clinicians may not need a formal test to determine a diagnosis for treatment planning. Even superb diagnosticians may neglect to ask key questions, and a survivor can evade detection. Although not universally true, many survivors steadfastly avoid any disclosure regarding traumatic events. In fact, those who minimize the connection the most, tend to be the most traumatized clients. Conversely, clients who tell you details, particularly in a detached manner, are more likely to be factitious clients.

During initial interviews, I tend to ask open-ended questions, such as "Are there any events that you can identify that were overpowering, where you felt out of control, and which might have some connection to what brings you into treatment?" Be reminded that simply identifying an event does not result in a PTSD diagnosis. An identifiable, recalled, or volunteered event is a start, but it does not make the diagnosis.

Dissociation can be another diagnostic obstacle. Clients in a dissociative state are not well organized in terms of thoughts, emotions, articulation, or expression. Dissociation, which includes the numbing response, is an effective, almost automatic protective mechanism. The clinician can easily confuse dissociative symptoms with depression, post-acute withdrawal, various neurological phenomena, arrogance, and narcissism. One highly symptomatic survivor might seem histrionic and prone toward exaggeration, whereas the next client might seem unemotional, disengaged, and "out of it."

Intuitive Factors in Identifying PTSD

Skilled clinicians can rapidly assess PTSD on the basis of intuitive factors. As clinicians, we are sometimes taught to "trust our gut" when determining PTSD during a routine consultation with a client. A clinician's intuitively derived diagnostic indicators must be tempered with logical and sound questioning. Never substitute intuition for logic. In general, the more rapidly you can make your assessment, the more rapidly you can begin your interventions. I view the first interview as an opportunity for the first clinical interventions. The more you can achieve early on, the stronger your clinical impact.

In terms of intuition, another word of warning is necessary. Many clinicians are survivors themselves and may see their own issues in clients. Do consult your gut, but also check out your hypotheses with careful, logical questions. There is no substitute for an integrated approach in assessing PTSD. In fact, this sets the tone for what we must do in terms of treatment. If we are too mechanical and precise, we miss the process. If we are only process oriented and use intuition, we can make huge errors. Emotional and cognitive integration is the gold standard for the superior clinician. Conversely, clinicians who function only by instinct are likely to get manipulated or perhaps even seduced by their needy clients. It is no accident that so much of the classic literature on borderlines focuses upon countertransference issues.

In terms of intuitive cues, clients who exhibit poor boundaries, excessive neediness, and profound detachment are possible trauma survivors. In addition, those who display extreme unevenness in mood may have this disorder. Let your gut help you in formulating your questions, but never make your decisions on instinct alone. Diagnosis, like therapy, is an art form, and an integrative one at that.

■ ■ ■

CHAPTER THREE

THE BIOLOGY OF PTSD MADE SIMPLE

Some clinicians love the mechanics of biology. However, many clinicians feel their knowledge of biology is inadequate, and when the topic is brought up, they experience anxiety and their eyes glaze over. The goal of this chapter is to help clinicians build the foundation necessary to understand and treat survivors of trauma. Some knowledge of biology is vital for treating trauma clients, particularly clients with addictive disorders who have considerable biological complications. Most addiction counselors do master some biological basics of the addiction process. Similarly, clinicians working with PTSD should have enough understanding to explain certain core aspects of biology that trauma survivors experience. For those who want more information, Babette Rothschild (2000) and Peter Levine (1997) can provide the reader with depth and detail.

The goal of this chapter is to communicate the very skeleton of what we now know about the biology of PTSD. No, you need not become immersed in the technical language, but a superior clinician can speak to all dimensions with enough information to provide clients with the necessary normalization, comfort, and encouragement. I gratefully acknowledge Don Catherall, Ph.D., for providing for me his synthesis of the biological factors. I borrow from his vision and have further simplified his material.

Clinicians need to know that traumatic events can affect biological systems, sometimes permanently. Specific hormonal balances may be changed, and some evidence suggests changes at a cellular level. For a traumatized client, the link between words and emotion can become disrupted. The executive area of the brain can no longer "speak" to the primitive areas. The primitive areas are sounding an ongoing alarm, and the survivor cannot use words or concepts to soothe himself or herself. In these circumstances, talking fails to soothe and can irritate a client who has been triggered. Knowing when to be silent and what is going on biologically will help the clinician better assist the client.

In this chapter, we will also briefly review medications that appear to help in the treatment of PTSD and CPTSD. There is no magic bullet, but medication can be a vital part of treatment. Having some awareness of what works can help clinicians in terms of coordinating the medical/psychiatric care that can make a huge difference in the lives of clients with PTSD.

Finally, I advocate the need for natural methods of biological intervention. Counselors need not provide this service and indeed should not unless specifically trained. However, advocating active pursuit of balanced eating, relaxation methods, physical exercise, and wellness activities can help almost any client, especially clients with co-occurring disorders such as PTSD and addiction.

Neuronal Responses and Disruption of Language

When something frightening occurs, we have two automatic messaging mechanisms that become active: a neuronal system and a hormonal system. The neuronal system is an information transmission system that uses the nervous system to send information to the brain and transmit signals from the brain to specific sites. A hardwired network sends information by electrochemical impulses. The neuronal response is almost instantaneous. For example, think about what would happen if you saw a bear in the woods. Would you think, "That is a big bear. I am in danger," and then run? Or would you become frightened automatically and run without thinking? Modern brain-scanning devices now show us that we react *before* we think. This is an incredibly adaptive part of our evolutionary wiring. Our bodies mobilize for action even before we know what is threatening us. Otherwise, it would take precious time to analyze the threat. Instead, our response is almost instantly intuitive and without higher thought.

Figure 5 provides us with a simple cross section of the brain. Note in figure 5, the lower, primitive area of the brain is called the limbic system, and the more advanced part of the brain is called the neocortex. The limbic system functions automatically and does not require conscious processing of information. The upper area, the neocortex, is what defines us as human beings. The neocortex gives us a sense of self. It is the core of higher-level information storage and processing.

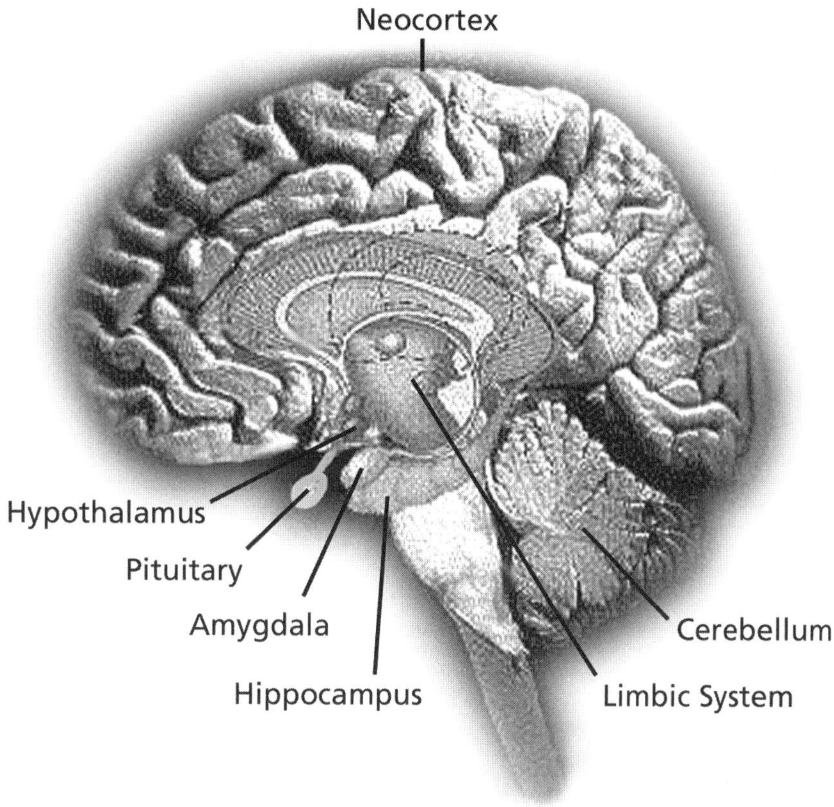

Figure 5

Returning to our consideration of a dangerous stimulus, information first goes to the lower part of the brain (the limbic system). One location, the amygdala, seems to be the command center for emotion, especially fear. It is interesting to note that the amygdala is next to the area of the brain associated with smell. Is this why we believe we can almost smell fear? The amygdala's proximity to the sense of smell may also explain why the sense of smell tends to be the most powerful emotional trigger. Many clients report the most powerful flashbacks occur with an olfactory stimulus.

The amygdala then affects the hippocampus, which is right next to it. The hippocampus is the gateway between higher levels of thought and lower levels of thought. Think of the hippocampus as the gate between thinking (the neocortex) and reacting (the limbic system). A frightening stimulus results in the inhibition of the hippocampus, causing a loss of access to words, new learning, and memory. A specific form of memory—declarative memory—is interrupted. It appears that traumatic events are stored in a different circuit from ordinary memory. This might explain why memory is uneven and may also explain blocked memory and repression. Thus, there appears to be a biological basis for memory disruption. Repression may be biological.

So, how does this information pertain to treatment? Traditional interventions rely on higher cortical function. Clinicians are experts in talk therapy. We reason, we discuss, we challenge, and we work on inner dialogue, belief systems, and cognitions. Most of what we are trained to do involves higher levels of cognitive processing. When a trauma survivor is triggered, higher levels of information processing go off-line. This fact may explain why survivors look as if they have entered an altered state. They stare ahead and seem dazed. They may not even see you there. Their eyes take on a haunting quality, sometimes referred to as "survivor eyes." They seem to look through you, not at you. Figure 6 is a classic painting, "Marines Call It That 2,000 Yard Stare," which illustrates the blank look of trauma.

Words do not seem to soothe someone who is profoundly triggered by trauma. The person must first get grounded, and this may involve simple interventions that do not rely on words, such as breathing, guided imagery, eye

Figure 6

movement desensitization and reprocessing (EMDR), and select forms of hypnosis. Some physical forms of intervention may be needed: Massage therapy, martial arts, yoga, tai chi, and self-defense training seem to activate individuals and give them new methods of mastering the instinct to freeze and stare. Some clinicians advocate touch, but this is contraindicated, in my opinion, due to the potential for misinterpretation, boundary violation, and potential lawsuits. Some programs use pets, specifically dogs or horses, to help clients manage fear and increase activation involving touch rather than words. One of the most effective treatment programs for World War II combat veterans with war neurosis was at Montrose VA Medical Center. Puppies were issued to the veterans, and they were an integral part of recovery. Part of what we learn from biology is that we may not be able to rely solely upon cognitive methods of intervention.

Hormonal Responses

The other information highway inside the body involves the hormonal system. The hormonal system relays information by flooding the body with powerful chemicals (hormones) that affect certain organs and the overall organism. The hormonal system is not hardwired and the chemicals involved tend to affect many systems at once. This system is slower and most often less precise than the neuronal system, but hormones have a potent effect, very often adaptive, but sometimes disruptive.

Stressful events result in the release of a hormone called cortisol. Cortisol (a glucocorticoid, essentially a hormone that affects the burning of sugar or glucose) is often referred to as the stress hormone. Some researchers once believed that trauma survivors had higher blood levels of cortisol. In fact, Rachel Yehuda (1990) made a simple but startling discovery. She found that the individuals with PTSD whom she examined had *lower* levels of cortisol. It is not precisely clear what this means, but one interpretation is that chronic stress wears down the chemicals in the brain, leaving symptomatic individuals in a chronic state of alarm and feeling "worn out." Hypervigilance seems to have a biological price. I have often used the analogy of an automobile alarm. Perhaps the first time a car alarm goes off, it serves a purpose. However, when any little bump or breeze occurs, it goes off again and gets tuned out, but at the same time it wears down your battery. In a similar fashion, it appears that chronic stress responses in the form of active PTSD can deplete one of the core glucocorticoids—cortisol.

Stress also stimulates the adrenal gland and the production of adrenaline and noradrenaline. However, current literature now refers to these two hormones as epinephrine and norepinephrine (this has confused many casual readers). Epinephrine (adrenaline) increases arousal and speeds up the burn rate of sugar. This increase in sugar gives an individual more energy and strength. The increase of epinephrine explains how a frail mother can suddenly become strong enough to lift a car in order to rescue her child.

Epinephrine results in sympathetic arousal. It produces the "fight" part of the energy surge following a threatening stress. This powerful hormone increases blood flow to the extremities, increases heart rate and respiration, improves reaction time, and slows down digestion. (Blood chemistry also changes so that our bodies, if injured, will heal more rapidly and not be as prone to bleeding to death.) So, sympathetic arousal (via epinephrine) makes you better prepared for a fight. Some of us are genetically disposed to produce more epinephrine when a stress or a threat occurs.

Norepinephrine (noradrenaline) has the opposite effect of epinephrine. It results in parasympathetic arousal. Too much norepinephrine can produce fear and feelings of helplessness. Fear has adaptive value; it teaches us to avoid conflict, run when necessary, and keep away from potentially dangerous things, like snakes. Many fears, including fear of snakes and heights, seem to be wired into our genes. You do not need words or learning to produce a fear response to certain stimuli. Extreme or sustained fear produces a flow of norepinephrine that results in dissociation. The surges of anxiety can even result in a loss of consciousness. A more complex question regarding breathing is not yet clear. We seem to slow down our breathing when we're the most fearful. This may have to do with the "going limp" response we see in captured mammals. This response may have some value when escape is not possible.

Dissociation, helplessness, and fear appear to be fueled by increased levels of the hormone norepinephrine, and we have parasympathetic arousal. One chemical (epinephrine) produces intense surges of energy; the other chemical (norepinephrine) produces fear and dissociation. We produce both of these hormones during times of threat, but the balance of these chemicals might affect how we behave.

One question we might consider: Are acts of heroism or cowardice a function of hormones? In other words, do those who act "bravely" feel fear but have a more dramatic sympathetic response and pump out epinephrine? Do those who flee or freeze, as do 25 percent of all soldiers in their first firefight, pump out more norepinephrine? This question is yet to be answered, but it does make you reconsider social judgments of people's behaviors. We may be looking at biochemistry, not just personality. I should also note that training, exposure, and conditioning affect how we behave and what we feel. We have to consider both chemistry (genetics) and environmental exposure (conditioning/training).

One other piece of minor but fascinating information: Recent research suggests that during times of danger, the stomach produces extra serotonin. In fact, there appears to be a serotonin circuit in the stomach that is independent of the brain. Thus, when we say, "I had a gut reaction," "I had that queasy, sinking feeling," or "I had butterflies in my stomach," we may be responding to a change in serotonin levels in the gut. It is possible that this gives the brain information on an independent or redundant circuit. "Trust your gut" may involve one of the key brain chemicals: serotonin. However, clinicians should not reinforce the directive "learn to trust your gut." This may be true for neurotics, but it is contraindicated for clients with PTSD and particularly those with CPTSD.

The glucocorticoids (and other stress-related neuropeptides) seem to affect the hypothalamus and, subsequently, the hippocampus. The hippocampus interacts with the amygdala, the fear center. Glucocorticoids tell the hypothalamus to chill out, unless the amygdala says danger is still present. The extra glucocorticoids appear to kill hippocampus cells. Therefore, the elegant balance between fear and thinking is disrupted. The hippocampus is the gateway between the primitive limbic system (amygdala or fear center) and the "higher order" of thinking and verbal parts of our brain (the neocortex). So, the ongoing hormonal imbalance may damage the anatomy. (There is also evidence to suggest certain cells in the amygdala are changed when we are exposed to prolonged stress.)

The net insight is that chronic stress seems to affect the neuronal circuitry and the hormonal circuitry and appears to damage actual organs and cells in the brain. Therefore, when a loved one says a person has changed after a traumatic event, there appears to be a biological underpinning to this observation. The delicate balance of systems that evolution developed to protect us appears to become unbalanced. So, we are dealing with a biological, biochemical set of changes, not just "fuzzy" psychological factors.

Prescription Medications

Medication can be a vital part of helping addicted clients with PTSD and CPTSD. No single medication ameliorates all of the symptoms of PTSD, but medications are invaluable. Some clinicians believe that medication is not good for clients with PTSD and that clients must learn to deal with their emotions naturally. Americans pop too many pills, a clinician may think. Addicts in particular seek relief by taking pills. This critique certainly had merit when the only medications available were the potentially addictive benzodiazepines (Valium and Librium). In fact, benzodiazepines were used to treat PTSD in early-era Vietnam combat vets, and sadly, many became addicted or displayed cross addiction. Clinicians who are skeptical of medication use may believe that if clients do not feel, they will not heal. This may have some truth, but this construct cannot be applied universally or recklessly.

On the other hand, many clients have endured nonproductive suffering and endless triggering, and some have attempted or completed suicide because medicines were not made an option. I have seen this occur with clients and family members. The clinician steadfastly adhered to the old idea of not interfering with the necessary intensity so that the client can feel, understand, and let go. In some respects, no pain, no gain. Whereas treatment cannot be an exclusively technical or cognitive process, excessive descent into despair can be dangerous, even lethal. As many survivors have said, "I never would have made it without the medicine." In general, the more severe the symptoms of PTSD, as in CPTSD, the more likely medications are indicated. Presently, we have many reasonably good medication options. They can help to save lives.

Selective Serotonin Reuptake Inhibitors

Selective serotonin reuptake inhibitors (SSRIs) can be incredibly valuable. PTSD and CPTSD clients often suffer from uneven mood, are vulnerable to severe bouts of depression, and often engage in obsessional thinking. In general, SSRIs do not dull the senses. They simply improve a sense of well-being and interrupt some of the debilitating effects of an alarm system that has become unbalanced. One colleague reassured her anxious client with the following feedback: "SSRIs are kind of like water wings. They keep you above the water line, but you still need to swim to shore." Table 2 lists some commonly used SSRIs and their generic names.

TABLE 2: SELECTIVE SEROTONIN REUPTAKE INHIBITORS (SSRIs)	
Brand Name	***Generic Name***
Zoloft	sertraline
Paxil	paroxetine
Prozac	fluoxetine
Celexa	citalopram
Lexapro	escitalopram oxalate
Luvox	fluvoxamine

Which SSRI works best for trauma clients? That is an idiosyncratic question. Zoloft was the first effective SSRI approved for the treatment of PTSD. Some clients fare better with Paxil since it seems to help with symptoms of anxiety. Prozac can be problematic since it tends to energize and can actually make some trauma clients feel more agitated and anxious. Then again, it can help for some, especially those who tolerate the higher doses and display severe symptoms of obsessive-compulsive disorder (OCD).

Finding the right SSRI is an art form and involves trial and error. A counselor should obtain a release of information and confer with a qualified psychiatrist. In general, the superior psychiatrists welcome a counselor's or therapist's input, feedback, and information. In an ideal circumstance, all parties would work together to find the best match and dosage. In my opinion, family physicians have neither the specialty training nor the clinical experience to find the necessary match of medication and client.

Newer Antipsychotics

The atypical neuroleptics or newer antipsychotic medicines can be very helpful in managing acute episodes of overload. When clients with more severe PTSD get triggered, the intrusive effects can cause profound disruption in functioning. Concentration becomes poor, intrusive thoughts and recollections become overwhelming, anxiety levels are off the charts, sleep patterns are disrupted, and suicidal ideation/rumination may follow.

Many clinicians and clients balk at the mention of an antipsychotic for trauma survivors. This concern has to do with stigma, numbing, and side effects.

TABLE 3: ATYPICAL OR NOVEL ANTIPSYCHOTICS (NEUROLEPTICS)	
Brand Name	***Generic Name***
Risperdal	risperidone
Seroquel	quetiapine fumarate
Zyprexa	olanzapine
Abilify	aripiprazole
Geodon	ziprasidone

However, short-term use of Risperdal, Zyprexa, Seroquel, or Abilify can provide rapid, non-addictive symptom relief. Table 3 lists some of the atypical antipsychotics (neuroleptics) and their generic names.

In most instances, the newer antipsychotics will be used at lower doses for a short period, a week or two, sometimes longer. They are among the few options for managing severe anxiety without risking addiction or initiating a relapse. These medicines affect both dopamine levels as well as serotonin levels. Used at the right time and dosage, these medications can save precious clinical time, provide relief, and build strength.

Klonopin

Klonopin is a slow-release benzodiazepine, which, according to many addiction professionals, falls in the "gray zone." It is a benzodiazepine but in low doses does not usually result in an addiction-potentiating high (as opposed to Ativan, which releases quickly into the bloodstream. Rate of release is considered a large factor in the addictive versus non-addictive nature of a substance). In some intractable cases of severe anxiety, the use of Klonopin may be appropriate. It is very hard to distinguish between drug-seeking and treatment-resistant anxiety. In my opinion, the use of Klonopin should be a tool of absolute last resort for a client with a history of addiction. The majority of addiction treatment programs, including my own, will not use Klonopin. Others do, but very conservatively. I am hopeful that some new tools for anxiety management will be available soon.

Miscellaneous Non-addictive Medications

Antihypertensives are medications designed to lower blood pressure. One type of antihypertensive, the beta-blockers, includes Inderal (propranolol hydrochloride), which has been used successfully for many years in treating phobias and other anxiety disorders. It tends to be short-acting and non-addictive. When used in specific situations, it can help break a conditioned anxiety response. This medicine requires supervision and should be combined with psychotherapy.

Inderal can help manage stressful situations, particularly if the therapist is guiding the client in breaking emotional obstacles or triggers. Inderal does not tend to work well with generalized anxiety. In addition, clients who suffer from low blood pressure may be at risk for postural hypertension, dizziness, or possible loss of consciousness when getting up too quickly from a prone or seated position. Inderal, if used consistently, can exacerbate depression, as can any of the beta-blockers. On a positive note, antihypertensives are not addictive.

BuSpar was initially approved as an antianxiety medicine and later used as an antidepressant. For a number of years, professionals debated which it was, and they now tend to say it is both. It is not terribly effective for many clients but does work for some.

Desyrel (trazodone) is one of the older antidepressants. It can have a mild soporific effect, and some psychiatrists use it to assist in anxiety management. Some psychiatrists have used very low doses sublingually to interrupt an anxiety attack.

Effexor (venlafaxine) is an antidepressant that works on both serotonin and norepinephrine. Considered a second-line tool by many, it can be helpful when SSRIs do not seem to help, especially if there is a history of cocaine or amphetamine dependence. It also seems to help clients with a history of ADD or ADHD coupled with depression and PTSD.

Cymbalta (duloxetine), a serotonin and norepinephrine reuptake inhibitor, is the newest addition to this group of medicines and appears to have considerable potential.

Mood Stabilizers

As we saw in chapter 2, PTSD involves affective dysregulation. Clients have a hard time managing their mood and can be hypersensitive, histrionic, and irritable. Among PTSD clients, a high incidence of cyclothymic and bipolar disorders appear. This may reflect the intersection of genetic loading and environmental triggers. The loading may not be as heavy, but intense or prolonged exposure to traumatic events seems to result in a greater probability for formal mood disorder. The association seems higher with CPTSD. Obviously, the possibility of a formal mood disorder does need to be considered. In all fairness, it is rather hard to miss. More often, we see clients who are not responding to SSRIs or have mood swings that are disruptive but not full-blown bipolar.

The conservative use of medications like Neurontin, Topamax, or Lamictal can dramatically improve a client's sense of stability and well-being. Not to be used capriciously, these medications are sometimes overlooked. The mechanisms of how they help are not clear. The mood-stabilizing features of anticonvulsants was a serendipitous discovery. Finally, the old gold standard, lithium, seems to be highly effective with classic bipolar. However, the latest trend in pharmacotherapy is the use of multiple agents, particularly for treatment-resistant symptoms.

Medications for Sleep Disruption

One of the most common problems for PTSD clients is loss of sleep. These individuals have difficulty falling asleep or staying asleep. Prolonged loss of sleep can result in confusion, mental dulling, and even psychotic symptoms. Disruption of a sleep pattern can be a medical emergency. Fragile or severely distressed clients have higher risk for relapse and are more prone to acting-out. For these clients, hypnotics are contraindicated. Although some are aggressively marketed as not having benzodiazepines in them, they are still quite addictive. For clients with co-occurring addictions, Sonata, Ambien, and Restoril are not appropriate choices. In most instances, the novel neuroleptics are helpful and so, too, are some of the tricyclics, such as trazodone. For some individuals, short-term use of antihistamines can be effective.

Natural Tools: Diet and Exercise

It would be negligent to omit powerful, natural options for managing the biological aspects of post-traumatic phenomena. Exercise is a natural antidepressant and can be a highly empowering endeavor. I need not delineate what is widely known: Exercise can boost mood, help the immune system, and improve clarity of thought. When exercising, a person's serotonin circuits are boosted, and many people feel an amazing sense of well-being. Some trauma survivors avoid exercise, maintaining perceived control by remaining stationary, invisible, or still. Others become addicted to exercise. This can be one of the "ripple effects" of PTSD and addiction. It is not unusual to find severe cases where there is an eating disorder, compulsive exercise, and multiple manifestations of addiction including major swings in sexual behavior, tending toward extremes.

Food can become a major tool for self-medication. Comfort foods do indeed lower anxiety. A secondary effect is that some sexual abuse survivors purposely gain weight in order to reduce the likelihood of being seen as a sexual object. The vicissitudes of carbohydrate metabolism add to swings in mood and behavior. The specifics of the effects of foods with different glycemic index loadings are beyond the scope of this book. However, I have found that clients with PTSD, CPTSD, and those in early recovery can benefit from working with a nutritionist and a fitness consultant. In many instances, these features are built into primary recovery programs. Nonetheless, actual implementation sometimes lags behind, and clinicians who are involved in post-primary care should advocate adjunctive attention to health, exercise, and diet. Omega-3 and omega-6 do appear to have some positive effect in terms of boosting mood. So, a diet with lots of fish may help boost the effect of an antidepressant, and for some it may ameliorate low-grade symptoms.

A word of caution: Some health food supplements are addictive and dangerous. It is now known that maj wong is almost the same as a benzodiezepine. Several years ago, a supplement called Blue Nitro resulted in weight loss and building of strength. It was the equivalent of a steroid and, before being banned, injured many, producing some rage-driven steroid addicts. The deleterious effects of ephedra are well documented, resulting in some tragic fatalities.

A good clinician will attend to, coach, and advocate for additional scrutiny around diet and exercise. I am not suggesting that we become experts in either of these fields, but they are vital, integral parts of a comprehensive recovery strategy. If we fail to think about biology, we may miss a major set of tools in assisting our clients. This is why I strongly advocate multidimensional thinking. In order to be better advocates, we must think in terms of what is going on biologically. Appropriate interventions by trained providers can make a huge difference in all the other areas we are trying to impact. Sometimes simply getting clients to walk when they become anxious or triggered can change breathing rhythms and interrupt symptoms.

New Frontiers

Improvements in medical scanning equipment, expansion of our understanding of brain function, and the validation of some vital facts have solidified the clinical and scientific foundations for trauma-based disorders. Recent studies have confirmed that memory is indeed a complex function and that traumatic events follow a different circuit than memory of ordinary events. Scanning equipment permits us to observe separate pathways, limbic and cognitive, when a traumatic event occurs. Although controversial in some circles, the reality of dissociation, memory blocking, and repression is becoming grounded in scientific and biological reality. Memory is fragile, malleable, long-standing, easily distorted, and vividly preserved. With ever-improving imaging technology, these once mysterious and at times contradictory phenomena will be better understood in the very near future.

Recent research suggests the highly publicized PTSD prevention system, critical incident stress debriefing (CISD), might not work and in some instances may make things worse. Whereas prevention of trauma-related disorders does not seem to occur with the CISD systems, there are some exciting developments in terms of prevention. One recent study demonstrated that when an individual is distracted by a simple visual-spatial task during a traumatic event, he or she is less likely to develop symptoms. Thus, distraction techniques may help protect the brain from the overpowering effect of a traumatic event. It may be that distraction, and perhaps multitasking, is a variable in some of the more powerful treatment techniques, such as eye movement desensitization and reprocessing (EMDR).

Roger Pitman et al. (2002) conducted a bold study attempting to block the onset of PTSD with a chemical intervention. Pitman administered propranolol to some traumatized individuals in an emergency room setting. He found that those in crisis who were given this medicine were significantly less likely to develop PTSD. Although this is a preliminary finding, it may well be that the propranolol kept anxiety levels down, preventing the onset of a conditioned response. However, it is also possible that the memory circuits were directly intervened upon.

Other researchers are studying more fundamental interruptions in the biological circuitry of memory formation, using specific proteins involved in memory formation. Another exciting discovery is that a specific type of serotonin,

5HT-1, seems to be involved with all anxiety disorders. It is possible that the current SSRIs (based upon serotonin 5HT-2) are helping indirectly and that a new class of 5HT-1-specific medicines will be developed. Targeting this circuit with non-addictive medicine would be a tremendous breakthrough in treating the full spectrum of anxiety disorders, including trauma-based disorders.

As with addictive disorders, there is never likely to be a chemical cure for PTSD. Biology is only one part of this complex picture. However, this era of rapid discovery, scientific confirmation, and validation of the biological reality of trauma-based disorders is a new frontier. Some exciting discoveries and new tools await us.

Health Consequences

It has long been observed that stress can have an effect on physical health. The mechanisms involved as well as the degree of involvement are unknown and/or controversial. Much has been written about the mind-body link and some good data supports a connection in terms of stress and physical health. We know that clients with trauma-related conditions are at higher risk for developing certain physical conditions. They are also prone toward more colds, vague pain, and somatic complaints. In part, this is why some of the early literature on hysteria and psychosomatic medicine came into being. Certain clients, particularly those with trauma issues, seem to have more frequent physical complaints. Previously assumed to be psychological or psychosomatic, these complaints may actually have a physical underpinning.

Some studies suggest that stress affects immunological balance. In fact, a whole new area of research, neuropsycho-immunology, replaces the less precise investigations associated with psychosomatic medicine. Although this area of research is still in its infancy, these studies may finally shed some light on this long-standing, elusive connection. Whereas it is not likely that stress directly causes a laundry list of illnesses (the actual data has been overinterpreted by some), there is likely a legitimate link, particularly in terms of immunological effects. Clinicians should be cognizant of the fact that trauma survivors tend to have a higher incidence of the following conditions: chronic fatigue syndrome (CFS), fibromyalgia, reflex sympathetic dystrophy (RSD), irritable bowel syndrome (IBS), lower back pain, as well as vague, multifocal somatic complaints. Some clients are more prone toward tension and migraine headaches.

Clients with a history of trauma do seem to be sick more often and longer than the average individual. It may not be simple malingering, drug seeking, or "conversion reaction." It may be that stress affects the immune system more directly than was ever suspected, resulting in a greater likelihood of certain illnesses. The range and scope of the connection between trauma history and frequency of illness will require a lot more study, and not surprisingly, we will likely see an elegant interaction between genetic vulnerability and stress exposure. Clarity of this connection has eluded us for the last one hundred years. The good news is that sophisticated technology will enhance our understanding of this fascinating connection.

In the interim, clinicians should be careful not to jump ahead of the data. For example, clients do not think themselves into getting cancer, but stress exposure may play a more direct role in certain diseases for certain individuals. Simply knowing that increased illness is a likely stress consequence may help ameliorate the invalidation that some clients experience in so many settings. As a mentor told me thirty years ago, "Just because you're hysteric doesn't mean you are not really ill."

■ ■ ■

CHAPTER FOUR

MYTHS, TRENDS, AND MISSING FACTORS IN THE TREATMENT OF TRAUMA-RELATED DISORDERS

In this chapter, we will explore myths and misconceptions regarding PTSD and CPTSD treatment. The first step toward an integrated clinical vision requires us to examine old beliefs that may contaminate our perceptions. Some of these beliefs, such as facilitating complete recall, catharsis, or regression, are leftover myths from prior clinical models. Other misconceptions revolve around the intensity of traumatic events, whether you need to be a survivor to treat survivors, and whether empathy or confrontation should be the clinical emphasis.

We will also consider the impact of trends upon clinical style and approach. To some extent, what is fashionable at a given time can powerfully influence what we do and how we treat PTSD and CPTSD. It is hoped that the reader will become less vulnerable to trends and more focused on balance, synthesis, and integration.

Finally, we will consider missing factors. This includes time, language, simultaneity, multidimensionality, and teleology (a component of spirituality). Don't be intimidated by these terms. They will become logical and clear as you complete this chapter.

Myths and Misconceptions

Consciously or unconsciously, clinicians are influenced by the beliefs that are the foundations of their original training. Some of these beliefs may have full or partial validity for some clients, but are completely misguided when applied to addicts with trauma-related disorders. Applying the wrong assumptions can be damaging to the client and frustrating to the clinician. It is amazing how persistent some of these misconceptions can be.

Misconceptions and common myths leading to confusion and lack of confidence in clinicians are listed and discussed below.

Myth 1: Catharsis Is the Main Goal

Contrary to tradition, catharsis—or the letting go and expression of feelings—is not a good clinical objective. Clinicians once believed that clients needed to recall their traumatic event and experience the feelings in order to let them go. The belief in catharsis is an outgrowth of Freudian tradition, Tavistock, Erhard Seminar Training (EST), and the zeitgeist of the 1960s and 1970s.

Part of the foundation for catharsis has to do with the assumption that bottled-up emotions must be expressed. Whether this is a residual effect of the Victorian era, the hydraulic underpinning of analytic theory, or other social dynamics, we can let theorists debate. This belief permeates our culture and clinical models. Many trauma-distressed clients themselves ascribe to this model. They feel miserable, don't understand why, and believe that they need to work on opening up. In many settings, a clinician in training was rated as to whether he or she was able to help a client vent his or her feelings. Tears were a great indicator.

The problem with this tradition is that it doesn't always work and in some instances can make a client worse. PTSD and CPTSD are not simple problems of repression (stuffed feelings) remedied by a good cry. Catharsis is a simplistic model that lacks clinical or scientific evidence and leads clinicians down the wrong path. A narrow-minded adherence to this myth hurts many clients. In simplistic terms, some clinicians are good at "opening up" the client but have no idea how to put the client back together. As a result, the client becomes a clinical Humpty Dumpty. Though many clients feel better after a good cry, many feel even more hopeless than before. Some clients dramatically decompensate, use, relapse, or act out. I have seen too many clients grace the insides of psychiatric or addiction inpatient programs when the cathartic goal has been misapplied. To put this in more traditional terms, we have regression in service of the ego, and we have regression that is not in service of the ego. If this model is misapplied with bad timing, a client further along the severity continuum is more likely to decompensate with catharsis.

Catharsis is still employed on an institutional level, although not as widely as during the late 1980s and early 1990s. Clients who do experience real relief, at least temporarily, may become addicted to the cathartic process. Intense catharsis can be a profound experience and may be self-reinforcing, fostering institutional or clinician dependence. In simplistic terms, the relief found in catharsis is similar to the relief you feel when you stop hitting your head against the wall. You may not be better off, but at least the pain stops. Intense cathartic events produce adrenaline, and like so many benign intense endeavors, there is the possibility of enjoying it too much. As noted in chapter 2, intensity can be self-reinforcing, and many trauma survivors are attracted to dangerous endeavors. Catharsis in and of itself is not a good clinical model or goal.

Myth 2: If You Treat the Underlying Trauma, the Addiction Will Take Care of Itself

This is an extension of the critique surrounding repression. In classic psychiatric thinking, addiction is the result of unresolved trauma, and if you treat the trauma, other symptoms, such as drinking or using, will disappear. Most addiction professionals know this is specious, or perhaps even delusional, but some classically trained mental health clinicians who do not have training in addiction continue to believe this myth.

We know that addicts, as a combination of genetic loading and environmental factors, cross an invisible line. Once this line is crossed, we absolutely must treat the addiction first. Yes, sequence is vital and so is timing. If the trauma part is neglected, there is a six-month window where relapse is very likely to occur. We must treat the addict first and then begin treating the trauma. In an ideal setting, treatment should be integrated and both conditions treated simultaneously.

It should be noted that there is a school of thought, steeped in scientific evidence as an outgrowth of social learning theory, that states people use chemicals as a means of dealing with emotions. The clinical model teaches the client new methods of coping. It is classically behavioral and seems effective with substance abusers, but not addicts. The danger is that addicts will attempt these methods as a way for them to continue their substance use. The core conditioning components of this model are indeed a part of relapse prevention. The technique may have merit as part of relapse prevention for addicted trauma clients, and could work for substance abusing clients, but is potentially harmful if used instead of a Twelve Step approach for those who are dealing with classic addiction or alcoholism. There is definite danger in missing the sequence and diagnosis. Half-measures can result in a fatal outcome with an addict. Some critics would argue that we run the risk of overdiagnosing addiction and placing a substance abuser into a Twelve Step treatment model. Whereas this has undoubtedly occurred, I am not aware of any fatalities by erring in the direction of overtreating or overdiagnosing a substance abuse problem as a substance dependence problem. However, I am aware of numerous fatalities and devastating consequences of the reverse error.

Myth 3: The Severity of the Event Is the Most Important Factor in Trauma Disorders

Some clinicians continue to make determinations based upon their own norms and judgment of the reported events. This is a dangerous trap and can lead to inaccurate assessment. I must admit that I learned this lesson vividly once I moved away from treating combat veterans to the larger, general population of survivors. Fortunately, I was graced with a dramatic case early in this transition that affected my thinking.

When I entered the private sector in 1986, I had a young patient, Jonathan, in his mid-twenties, who had many features of anxiety. He was insecure, isolated, and suffered from severe self-doubt. Many clinicians had tried to assist him, but his symptoms continued. I was looking for an event of a traumatic nature. I thought that his symptoms fit PTSD. I did my usual rigorous history during clinical intake. I asked Jonathan if he could identify when he began feeling intense fear. Eventually, he recounted an incident that happened when he was six years old: The neighbor's German shepherd attacked Jonathan's precious pet bunny, biting its head off right in front of young Jonathan's eyes. When I heard this, I had some internal responses. I thought instantly that this was absurd. How could witnessing a bunny rabbit dying qualify as a traumatic event? I had spent years listening to horrific war-related events, and this story sounded so absurdly trivial in comparison. I quickly realized that this story occurred when Jonathan was six, not eighteen. This exposed my own bias, and ever since then I have learned to respect the perception of the observer. It is the *perception* of the event, not the event itself, that is most important in determining trauma-related disorders. Yes, age does matter.

Myth 4: Teaching Clients to Connect with Their Instincts Is a Vital (Initial) Part of Trauma Treatment

As we learned in chapter 2, clinicians need to utilize instinct as part of the diagnostic process. We are taught to "trust our gut" and most of us are trained to teach this to our clients. However, instructing clients to trust their gut can be ill advised for trauma clients in early recovery. Chapter 3 makes this logical: The limbic system is in charge when a client is triggered. Telling the client to calm down and trust your gut is analogous to telling an addict with cravings to listen to or trust his or her instinct to use. Interestingly, relapse urges and fear-based intrusions, which can include flashbacks and dissociation, all seem to involve the limbic system. The problem for triggered clients is that their gut tells them the wrong thing: Run, shut down, self-medicate, act out, destroy, dissociate, and trust nobody, including the clinician.

So, the well-intended universal advice of relying on instinct when applied to triggered clients is telling them to listen to their limbic system, precisely the opposite of what they need to know and hear. Instead, it is usually more appropriate and clinically effective to tell them, "Don't listen to your instincts when you are triggered. Your instincts are usually great, and they have protected you from harm. However, when your mood switches suddenly, especially in early recovery, do not listen to those urges, automatic messages, or instincts. It is likely that you are being bullied by the limbic system. It wants to protect you, but it is setting off a chain of reactions that shuts down your thinking and distorts your judgment. Instead of trusting your gut, activate your objective self, your higher levels of thought and consciousness. Slow down. In fact, while you are in early recovery, I strongly encourage you to designate a couple of core people with whom you can check out your accuracy. These people can include a sponsor, healthy peers in recovery, healthy family members, AA participants, and the therapist. So, do not listen to your gut. Instead, listen to the people whom you selected to help keep your judgment objective and balanced."

I also explain to clients how they can recognize when they have been triggered: a sudden, dramatic shift in mood and sense of safety. Very often, it is a shift toward sudden irritability or anger. In fact, I instruct many clients in advance to remember that when they feel these sudden surges of anger, chances are they have been triggered by something that made them feel threatened and this represents a likely distortion. They need to ask their "executive committee" if they have been endangered or triggered. Managing the distortions of the limbic system is a vital part of recovery. They need to learn to empower the neocortex, their higher levels of consciousness, and not let the limbic system continue to distort reality. I sometimes give clients the following simple phrase in written form, a kind of recitation or reminder in case of a crisis:

"Trust your brain, and quiet down the gut." I advise them that when they feel suddenly and intensely angry, talk to a peer, therapist, or sponsor about their reactions.

Myth 5: Only a Survivor Can Treat a Fellow Survivor

Not true. I have successfully treated addicts, combat veterans, and sexual abuse survivors. Early in my career, I was fortunate not to qualify as a survivor. I had certain advantages and certain disadvantages by not being a direct member of the "survivors club." It is a myth that you can help only if you have been through the experience. Be totally honest about your status if asked. Never pretend or avoid an honest response to this question with a survivor. Honesty is a far more important qualifier than history. Integrity, balance, empathy, and attentiveness also matter.

Myth 6: A Clinician Needs Only to Provide Empathy or Unconditional Positive Regard

The Beatles best summed it up with "All you need is love." This principle is a wonderful ideal, and I must admit, I am disposed to it. It is my most natural tendency and clinical default. (I had strong Rogerian training early in my career.) However, I have found that this principle of unconditional positive regard is not correct when working with survivors, particularly if they are dually diagnosed. The problem is you can enable them, make them weaker, and endanger them by applying only the principle of unconditional positive regard. Empathy alone does not empower and can result in the clinician reinforcing all kinds of distortions. In addition, a triggered client in early recovery is likely to crave or seek drugs.

Our job is to help question, not just provide support. These are very wounded and complex clients. Yes, they seek reassurance, empathy, and unconditional positive regard. However, their level of need tends to be limitless, and if you are thinking only in the Rogerian dimension, you will be manipulated, misled, and ultimately rejected for failing the empathy challenge. Do not give away your clinical objectivity to the illusion—no matter how appealing—that all they need is love and empathy.

Myth 7: Confrontation Is All You Need

Some addiction treatment models encourage an extremely confrontational clinical style, especially with difficult clients. Part of the assumption is that we are dealing with denial, narcissism, and a sense of entitlement. While there may be truth to these assertions, the application of unbalanced confrontation can result in a poor outcome.

Some clinicians become intoxicated with power and apply confrontation techniques to "whip resistant clients into shape." This became part of an institutional paradigm; fortunately, the popularity of these techniques seems to be diminishing. I view these approaches as dangerous distortions of the Twelve Step model. These programs, again well intentioned, operate from the narrow perspective that relapsing clients need strong structure, guidance, and discipline. Clinicians who use confrontational techniques believe clients need to be told what to do and shouldn't be coddled or enabled. They tend to take military training principles and apply them to resistant clients. "We have to break them down first and then rebuild them." This boot-camp mentality can be effective and may have some applicability to some clients; however, it is contraindicated for trauma survivors.

Interestingly, this approach appears to work temporarily for survivors. Because survivors know how to survive, they go underground until the pressure is off and identify with the aggressor, at least until it is safe. Sadly, many clients have been further damaged with this approach. Some addicts' and victims' behavior needs confrontation, but not the extreme practice that can result in shame-based compliance, which makes clients more disturbed. Some clients have been more traumatized by unbalanced, highly confrontational tactics than by the original trauma.

Fortunately, this model no longer dominates, but the simplistic seduction of this model continues to place survivor clients in countertherapeutic circumstances. Know your resources, both institutions and individual clinicians. Matching client to model is imperative in this population.

Remember, severely distressed clients will see any confrontation of behavior as a personal assault. They will report to family or others that they are being harassed or abused. Do not confuse a client's over-hypersensitivity to feedback with the overapplication of confrontation to which I am referring. Some of our clients may perceive aggression, invalidation, and rejection when to the objective observer these are not present. I have seen highly symptomatic clients who were given gentle feedback they did not wish to hear manipulate enmeshed providers. These clients claim abuse where none has occurred. Remember, this client population is hypersensitive, prone toward extremes of perception, and nihilistic, seeking to defeat the most balanced intentions of clinician and institution alike.

Myth 8: "Just Get Over It"

This variant is best expressed by the following sayings: Pull yourself up by the bootstraps; Get off the pity pot; Stop feeling sorry for yourself; Grow up; and Take responsibility. This approach can be countertherapeutic, insensitive, or abusive, particularly with survivors. Interestingly, some survivors seek out this negative feedback. No, this is not masochism. Instead, it validates their low self-esteem. "Ah, somebody finally confirmed what I knew all along. I am a loser." This same dynamic results in recapitulation of the trauma and selection of partners who will reject or abuse. Survivors in early recovery seek enabling and invalidation, but need warmth and honest feedback instead. We are seeking gradations, not extremes. It is incredibly tempting to lose patience with a client engaging in victim behavior. However, there is nothing more invalidating than being patronizing.

I once observed a world-renowned expert in PTSD do a forensic interview with a client. He was working for a legal defense team, protecting the doctor, and therefore he was looking to deny the client's condition. The client knew this in advance and was well prepared to tell her story with poise and objectivity. The expert interviewed her for four hours, listening respectfully but clearly trying to find other diagnoses. The expert was an older person who had a physical handicap. The client was traumatized as a result of a medical condition. At the end of the interview the expert, apparently feeling guilty for his lack of empathy, said to the client: "I have been through worse things than you, and I got over it. Just put the memories from the front of your brain into the attic. You'll get over it." This well-intended, but mistimed closing statement sent the client into an emotional spin. The expert's words may have had validity, but his timing and lack of sensitivity couldn't have been worse.

Myth 9: Our Primary Goal Is to Change Behavior

This statement is more of a misconception than a myth. Indeed, the goal of any therapy is to facilitate behavior change. However, with trauma-based disorders the goal is much simpler, yet profound. Our primary goal is to facilitate self-acceptance. Self-invalidation is part of the core dynamic that facilitates victim thinking and behavior. If we focus on behavior change and miss the overarching issue of self-acceptance, we are not fully serving the client, particularly those at the more complex end of the spectrum.

Trends in PTSD Treatment

It is not a startling declaration to note that clinical theory, technique, and applications are prone to trends. This applies to addiction treatment as well as mental health treatment. To some extent, the evolution in models can be healthy; our fields should never become stagnant. However, there has been a tendency for rapid swings driven more by fashion than objectivity or science. I am amazed by the incredible power of trends in determining how to treat trauma survivors. I suspect this is related to the seemingly daunting task of treating a phenomenon so new, incredibly complex, and mercurial. I have seen many treatment trends touted then discarded. Most were benign, but some caused significant damage, particularly when misapplied or zealously applied.

In the early 1980s, the dominant PTSD treatment model essentially said survivors, specifically combat veterans, needed to speak with peers. Both individual and group options (the rap session) were seen as the path to recovery. The core construct was that trauma survivors needed to grieve, remember, feel, and recover. It was an abreaction, catharsis model, but one that encouraged group therapy and an outpouring of feelings. One variation was the rap group facilitated by a Ph.D. psychologist using marijuana as a tool for calming down veterans and helping them manage anger. It does not take a genius to discern the noxious consequences of this practice, but for a period it was very popular.

Subsequently we had many variations of the "let it out" theme. Gestalt therapy was very popular and intensely dramatic. We also had a neoanalytic model with some dedicated practitioners. Psychodrama, similar to Gestalt, had a long run of popularity and is still touted as the best method of treatment by at least one facility. Flooding techniques were applied early on, but it became clear that there were significant hazards involved. Classic conditioning methods were modified using systematic desensitization as per Joseph Wolpe.

As the acceptance of trauma-related phenomena grew, the focus on retrieving repressed memories followed. Hypnosis was used, and in some rare instances the old "truth serum" (sodium pentathol) technique was used. The quest for the holy grail of complete recall, particularly when hypnosis was used, resulted in distortion of recall, false memories, or implanted memories.

This trend nearly invalidated the entire endeavor. Memory retrieval became and remains an anathema. Huge lawsuits occurred and some practitioners, including one highly competent colleague, were swept up in litigation. In the instance of the competent colleague, the charges were false, but the media exposure resulted in his becoming a victim of the press and the courts. He could no longer treat clients with any semblance of post-traumatic stress. Certainly, far more clients than clinicians were casualties of this trend. Creative exercises, including nondominant handwriting and recall, caused many clients to confabulate events and perpetrators. Rather than healing, many clients became victims of trend and technique.

One example of a client becoming a victim of a trend concerned a colleague, Mark, who was a combat veteran and addiction counselor seeking relief from the intrusive symptoms of his war experiences. He participated in a therapy group in the late 1980s. The Gestalt-style group was highly confrontational and pushed its members toward complete, gut-wrenching disclosure and expression. Of the original thirty-eight members, six committed suicide, directly or indirectly, as a consequence of their therapy. Going into the group sober, the vast majority relapsed. Mark recently told me, "I just ran into a guy from the group in 1991. He only has three months sober. You can see the damage they did." He added, "I suffered from dissociation for two years and did not even know what the hell was going on." Today Mark tells his story to sponsees, speaks at meetings, and has become an advocate for a more balanced, conservative, and integrative approach to treatment. Mark states that it took him at least ten years to recover from the "therapy," and he very nearly joined his deceased peers.

The last ten years have seen a trend toward the power techniques, which we will review in chapter 6. There has been enormous controversy over the power techniques, which includes eye movement desensitization and reprocessing (EMDR). Although abating, these techniques have caused a huge split of perception among providers. Many believe that these techniques provide astounding results; others view them as the victory of hype over objective science.

The most recent general trend has been incorporating some derivatives of recent medical scanning technology. The goal has been to intervene with techniques that will assist the client with the biological imbalances noted in chapter 3. Thus, there has been a trend toward touch therapy. Some of these techniques are reviewed in the next chapter. Some followers of this trend have made a contribution, but in some settings touch therapy has resulted in "crossed boundaries." I do not recommend that clinicians or primary caregivers violate boundaries by using techniques based on Rolfing, Gestalt, or any technique involving direct touch. Empowerment with movement-based interventions like tai chi, massage therapy with a properly credentialed provider, and more aggressive martial arts can be very therapeutic. I do advocate the use of animals as a means of facilitating the touch aspect where the quest is to "reset the amygdala," the stated goal of the biologically minded stress specialists. Again, the use of pets or equine therapy requires careful selection and incorporation and should not be suggested impulsively. Know your resources and your providers. These adjunctive therapeutic tools can be extremely helpful. However, do not misinterpret the trend and begin doing Gestalt exercises with your client.

Another subtrend has been the movement away from "open-ended" techniques and toward "protocol-driven" interventions. In my opinion, this reflects the dialectic of structure versus freedom. There is increased safety using the structure of the protocol-driven techniques. EMDR, for example, has definite safety mechanisms built into the structure and technique. This protects client and technician from some of the problems of the extreme open-ended paradigm where clinicians would ask broad questions in the quest for lost memory. The more complex client needs clinical artistry combined with solid technique. This is not as daunting as it might sound.

Trends in Addiction Treatment

In terms of addiction treatment, many gurus and trends have come and gone. Confrontation and regression were also themes in the world of addiction treatment. Some model and movement trends utilize tough love and even regression therapy. There were programs that put clients in diapers, insisting that the recalcitrant addict needed to be reparented. (This model has been applied to delinquent adolescents as well; however, a recent episode resulted in a fatality when program staff attempted to restrain and rebirth a child.)

Timing Trends for Addiction Treatment

Inpatient addiction treatment began as a one-year endeavor and shortly thereafter the model became ninety days. The twenty-eight-day treatment standard actually came about as a function of insurance. Blue Cross and Blue Shield of

Minnesota set the level at thirty days, and subsequently shifted to twenty-eight days. During the last ten years, managed care has intruded and pushed for shorter lengths of stay and outpatient treatment. This has been a devastating trend for many. Too many clients receive either the wrong level of care or too short a time in a residential or inpatient milieu. A distorted trend in the name of cost containment has reduced the size of the industry and demoralized many providers.

Trends in Mental Health

In terms of the overall mental health world, many techniques and models have evolved, peaked, and then fallen into obscurity. To name a few, we had the Ericksonian movement, neurolinguistic programming, and the Feingold diet.

It would take an entire volume to recount the many psychological treatment trends that graced the 1980s and 1990s. However, the mental health world is attempting to catch up to the intuitive and inspired brilliance of the Twelve Step paradigm. The world of mental health moved away from Freudian mysticism to scientific objectivism. The first step was the behaviorist revolution of the 1960s; it seemed all problems could be resolved by applying simple conditioning paradigms. Operationally defined, no problem was insoluble. Biofeedback provided hope that these techniques could provide amazing mastery of medical as well as emotional management. It did not take long for the limits of a strict behavioral model to be discerned, despite the plethora of research supporting the original constructs. It became obvious that people are more complex. We are social creatures with the ability to conceptualize and think.

We then "discovered" the cognitive-behavioral model. This model is considered the most valid for treating a wide range of conditions, including post-traumatic phenomena. Marsha Linehan, faced with the incredible challenges of the so-called borderline, incorporated a spiritual component to her model, dialectical behavior therapy (DBT). The introduction of Eastern thought has been immensely helpful to clients and clinicians. It is only within the last ten years that the mental health community caught up with the AA paradigm, which from day one included the spiritual domain. Perhaps the missing piece in the DBT model is the incorporation of addiction treatment. This requires a second language, if you will, spoken simultaneously with the behavioral change model represented in DBT.

This brief discussion of trends is not meant to be a rigorous and comprehensive review of the history of treatment models. My goal is to make the reader sensitive to the fact that we have been longing for a cure, a quick fix, and a comprehensive model. Are we there yet? Not really, but in my opinion, we can approximate the best fit even while the research continues.

Missing Factors

Over the years, I have taken for granted some factors that other clinicians omit or fail to consider. These missing factors include time, language, and simultaneity. Understanding these simple but powerful factors will provide you with a significant clinical advantage. The specific manipulative agenda of addicts with trauma-related disorders will also be revealed. We will then progress to the complex-sounding, but surprisingly simple issue of multidimensional assessment and therapy. Finally, a very obscure term, teleology, once understood and included, can substantially enhance your clinical impact.

Time

As they say in AA meetings, "Time takes time." Many clinicians and survivors seem to forget this simple wisdom. Survivors, especially when triggered, have many distorted perceptions, including their sense of time. During a crisis, time seems to slow down (an effect duplicated by cannabinoids). Subsequently, time can get lost during the fugue that follows. Some clients report a loss of days, weeks, and in some rare instances even years. Dissociation is clearly part of this process. After the acute crisis abates, survivors tend to avoid emotions and, to some extent, avoid dwelling in the present. They are either living in the past, when triggered, or in some ill-defined fantasy of the future, usually with catastrophic events anticipated. (This is part of the sense of foreshortened future, a ubiquitous feature of anxiety disorders.)

On a conceptual level, time may also go through a splitting process. Symptomatic clients live not in the middle (here and now) but in the past or future, both of which are based on fear or terror. Many interventions and techniques articulate the time distortions involved in traumatic aftermath. Some models actually describe the goal of therapy as *presentification,* that is, facilitating the client to live in the here and now. Indeed, this has some bearing on the AA wisdom of not projecting into the future. Facilitating a client to live in the here and now is one aspect of the time issue.

Another key aspect of time involves how long it takes to recover. Most survivors want immediate relief. New clinicians sometimes feed into this notion by providing unrealistic expectations: "This technique will make you much better." One of the most salutary interventions a clinician can make is telling the truth about recovery for both addiction and trauma-related disorders; it is a lifelong process.

During the early 1970s the Kübler-Ross paradigm gave the illusion of a logical, sequential grieving process. Some theorists declared that grieving must take place within a nine-month period following the loss. Any longer, and you were deigned a "pathological griever." Fortunately, this distorted clinical thinking was transitory. More enlightened theorists declared that grieving is a personal process that takes much more time and that a significant loss involves a process of about a five-year duration. One may never fully recover. I strongly emphasize the elucidation of the time issue. It takes clarity and repetition since most survivors do not hear this the first time through. I have found myself repeating the expectation of a long—if not lifelong—healing, adjustment, acceptance, and transcendence process. An accurate expectation of the healing process can relieve a tremendous amount of tension and angst. The frustration of not getting over the pain short-circuits logic. Time takes time and healing takes time. The fantasy of instant relief must be confronted and neutralized. Regularly reminding clients that healing will take a lot of time is as powerful as applying the first definition of PTSD. When the clinician helps normalize a client's trauma, and then helps correctly "set the clock," a far more stable foundation is established.

Language

The language used for addicts and survivors is similar, yet different. The Twelve Step paradigm has helped innumerable addicts, many of whom are survivors. It has initiated a healing process in which some clients can work through survivor issues without separate or additional therapy. A superb example of this is *Glory Denied,* the story of the longest-held P.O.W. of the Vietnam era, Jim Thompson. His was a tragic story, punctuated by childhood abuse, alcoholism, captivity, and prolonged torture. His last ten years were far healthier, despite ongoing tragedy. He got better not with formal therapy, but in AA rooms.

Conversely, a true alcoholic, one who has crossed that invisible line via genetics, environment, or self-medication, is not likely to stay sober without incorporating, formally or informally, a Twelve Step foundation. It is possible to get sober without formal intervention, or Twelve Step work, but it is indeed rare to find anyone who stops drinking because he or she had an emotional breakthrough or EMDR assisted him or her in managing acute symptoms. We can let the theorists debate this for years to come, but we clinicians need to accept the basics from what we observe. Quite simply, we cannot fix a multi-dimensional problem with a one-dimensional tool.

More important, the clinician must be cognizant of the fact that the inner dialogue of the survivor and addict is different. Again, we are talking about the same person, just different operational language. The language of addiction may simply say: "I need to get high. I want relief. I want to experience pleasure. I am not really an addict and I can handle it." Simultaneously, the language of the survivor might say: "I am bad. I don't deserve for things to go well. It is boring, and I need challenge. I need to prove to the world I am unworthy. I found out I was unworthy when I failed to control events." If the clinician or counselor only speaks to the addict, a key portion of the inner language is missed. In fact, if the survivor is addressed and the addict ignored, or vice versa, the omitted portion tends to become righteously indignant. The client whose survivor issues are ignored may react negatively and say, "The counselor really doesn't understand me. I am different, and I must show it." Conversely, the clinician who is only speaking to the survivor tries to soothe and use the best techniques available but may miss the inner dialogue of the addiction disease, which may say, "Wow. This is cool; look how hard they're working to fix me. Now we can get away with some shit and just have a little fun. Now that I feel a bit better, I know I can use just a little, and use like an Earth person."

Failing to speak to both sides of the client's issues regarding addiction and trauma will leave enough room for either illness, disease, condition, phenomenon, process, or whatever we label it to cause regression, relapse, or self-invalidation. Don't make the mistake of speaking only one language. You need not be fluent in both. You can divide the responsibility, but both voices—the addict's and the victim's—must be heard. A superior clinician will have the wisdom to recognize the difference.

Simultaneity

When to treat which condition can be vexing issues for co-occurring disorders. Not only do we need to contend with timing, but also we must factor in severity, needs of the individual, and intended design of a treatment program. Clients with trauma-related disorders who are also addicts would ideally have both treatments occurring at the same time. However, few facilities are able to do both at once.

In a twenty-eight-day primary addiction treatment program, the emphasis should be upon the addiction, but trauma issues should be identified. Too early an emphasis on trauma treatment can distract the client, feed into milieu chaos, and undermine necessary incorporation of the disease model of addiction. Simply treating the PTSD next, without ongoing Step work, is also contraindicated. After the basics of addiction are at least partially mastered, the next phase of treatment should provide rigorous elements of both Twelve Step work and active trauma treatment. Splitting the tasks can result in confusion or poor outcome. The intensity and formality of ongoing care must match the perceived intensity of distress. Less severely impacted clients can go home and continue the simultaneous work on an outpatient basis. The most disturbed trauma client may require a second inpatient treatment where the emphasis is on trauma while Twelve Step work is rigorously continued. For clients in the middle, or those who have done both primaries, an extended residential, transitional treatment program can be a lifesaver. Making these determinations early on is part of the art form of diagnosis and is very much dependent upon the clinician's perception of severity. In my experience, the trauma portion has been often overlooked, denied, neglected, or minimized.

The general error is doing too little rather than too much. Intensely injured addicts need intensive care, intelligently coordinated and provided with simultaneity. Ideally, there should be enough structure and continuity to protect clients from the internal and external chaos of their addiction and posttraumatic dynamics.

Understanding the Game

I came to the realization that many clinicians have little idea that they are part of a larger manipulation. I was invited to train clinicians for a county agency. I asked what they needed most, and I was told that the clinicians were becoming "burned out on borderlines." It became obvious to me that severely traumatized clients were continuing to get what they sought: rejection. The county counselors had almost no awareness that they were being manipulated by survivor dynamics. It was amazing to see the transformation in clinicians' attitudes as we reviewed the basics. As I described the inner dynamics of repetitive self-invalidating behavior, many clinicians volunteered case examples that they had misunderstood. Yes, this is a huge reframing. Clinicians are not just getting burned out on borderlines; they do not realize that on an unconscious level, many survivors want to be told they are hopeless. In fact, I view this desire to be so powerful that I coined a term describing it. I refer to it as "born-again nihilism." It is the antithesis of spirituality, but clients try to "spread the word." Most clients find humor in this term. Recognizing this missing piece is a vital component of an accurate, integrated vision of what we are seeing. It is indeed a part of the first step toward integration.

Multidimensional Assessment and Therapy

In medicine and mental health, we are witnessing a trend toward using multiple therapies to treat intractable disorders. Millions of lives were saved with the utilization of an AIDS cocktail as opposed to a single medicine. More recently, this principle is being applied to the treatment of cancer: Use several classes of chemotherapy to fight the disease. As one of the oncologists I conferred with stated, "It makes no sense to hold back tools in reserve; we hit this disease with everything we have, and the outcomes are better."

The use of a multidimensional strategy of conceptualization and psychotherapy is not new. It has been part of charting and record keeping for decades and is part of the tradition most clinicians received in training: the biopsychosocial model. Arnold Lazarus (1989) introduced multimodal therapy, and it was immensely popular for a brief time. Theodore Millon (1983) introduced a disciplined and rigorous format for conceptualizing psychopathology. In *Modern Psychopathology,* Millon went through the diagnostic categories and described each problem in terms of biology and environment. It was such an impressive work, and such a powerful conceptual model, I can remember one supervisor saying that if he was stranded on a desert isle and had to choose one or two books he could take, Millon's text would definitely be one.

Sadly, in application, many clinicians forget the power and wisdom of a multidimensional framework for assessment and therapy. In a graduate school assignment, we were asked to role-play a disorder while the class provided a diagnosis. I played a diabetic whose sugar fluctuations were causing cognitive and behavioral changes. Since this was not anticipated, it was missed by most of my peers.

In terms of therapy and assessment, many practitioners become comfortable with the model and dimension of their training. I strongly advocate a daily application of multidimensional thinking.

I visualize a four-dimensional grid, figure 7, and methodically comment on each of the dimensions (psychological, spiritual, biological, and interpersonal) for each session. In fact, I find that I must remind myself before each session to see all of the dimensions and hear the client through all four filters. (I use the grid to help keep my balance; I try to keep my "gyroscope" right in the middle and not let the intensity of what I hear pull me off balance.) It is amazing how much more you will see, hear, and comment upon. In addition, the rigor of your thinking will help reassure your client.

Teleology

Teleology is a word from philosophy that refers to the final objective or destination. It is from the Greek word *teleos* meaning final destination and

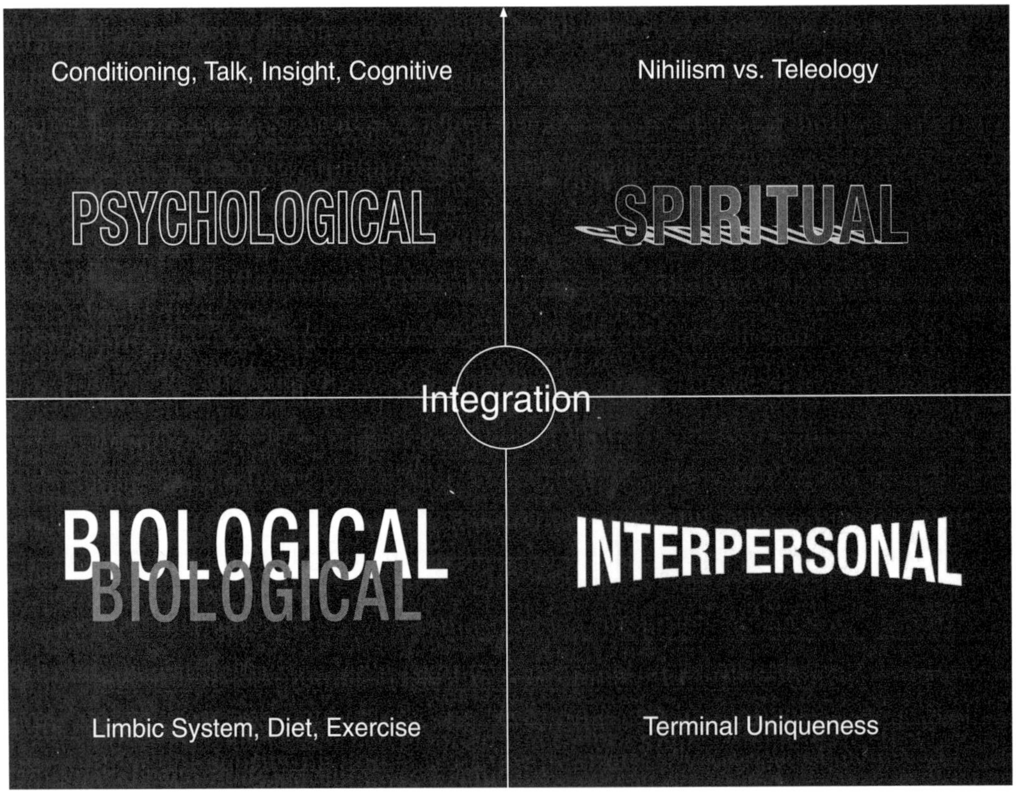

Figure 7

describes a philosophical style. Viktor Frankl's classic work *Man's Search for Meaning* emphasized the power of teleology. Frankl observed that in the Nazi concentration camps, those who had a vision of where they wanted to be, and held on to that hope, tended to survive when others perished. Clearly, the vision of a future event did not control destiny. However, if a person "gave up," the probability of death increased. As the famous quote goes: "Man can live thirty days without food, three days without water, but not one second without hope."

Veterans of Bataan and other horrific circumstances of torture verified Frankl's observation about hope, and more specifically about the power of teleology. Prisoners would literally declare their time of death. This seemingly mystical phenomenon of saying it is time for me to give up believing and hoping can result in rapid decline and death. It is not mystical, but simply the way it is. We have an incredible need for a future vision, and we thirst for hope. Without hope, we are likely to perish. As Primo Levi stated, "The aims of life are the best defense against death."

Teleology is a powerful part of the spiritual domain. It may be the most powerful component. Having a belief in God is often associated with teleology, but it is not absolutely essential. In fact, the concept of teleology as applied by Frankl—psychological, philosophical, spiritual, and personal vision—taps into a uniquely powerful part of our reality. Humans do seek spiritual inspiration, and teleology may be a key factor in helping guide a victim out of the chaos.

Teleology is a powerful but forgotten concept. I use teleological principles with almost all survivor clients. As delineated in the next chapter, I use it from the very first session. In my opinion, it is the most important missing factor, particularly for clients suffering from more severe trauma disorders. More information about teleology can be found in chapter 6.

■

An integrated clinical vision is invaluable when treating addicted clients suffering from trauma-related disorders. An overemphasis on a single dimension or technique can set up clinician and client for failure. In general, addicts with co-occurring PTSD have more severe trauma histories. All clinicians need to consider how therapy is timed and where it is delivered, as well as the clarity of language and clinical goals. Our clinical expectations, sometimes more than technique, can affect outcome. I hope the reader will learn to speak the languages of recovery and PTSD, avoid repetition of misguided techniques, and incorporate the range of thinking needed for a multidimensional viewpoint.

CHAPTER FIVE

TECHNIQUES FOR TREATING TRAUMA DISORDERS

Treating trauma-related disorders can be very complex. Making it more difficult is the vocabulary and different models, techniques, approaches, tools, and methods that can be used. In order to simplify this maze, we will review a variety of techniques in this chapter. These techniques can be used with or without a particular theoretical model. Some are simple and helpful; others are countertherapeutic. Ultimately, the clinician must have some familiarity with the range of options in order to make his or her own clinical synthesis. Exposure to this range of techniques can facilitate a first step toward clinical integration.

Breathing

Perhaps the most powerful and simple technique you can teach to clients with a trauma-related disorder involves breathing control. Exposure to danger causes an increase in respiration. Rapid breathing tends to be temporary. Clients with PTSD and CPTSD almost universally suffer from shallow breathing, particularly when triggered. Why this occurs is not clear, but it may have something to do with hyperalertness, waiting to hear if danger is indeed forthcoming. Whatever the explanation, reduced respiration results in an increase of carbon dioxide in the blood and a decrease in oxygen availability. When this happens, clients will breathe with great rapidity but in a shallow manner. They hyperventilate. This is what happens with a panic attack or anxiety attack. Breathing too deeply and too rapidly, or breathing too shallowly, can also result in a temporary high. Some individuals report mystical experiences when baseline-breathing rhythms are off balance.

You can help clients master their anxiety by simply teaching them to breathe slowly with the diaphragm (diaphragmatic breathing). There is nothing really complicated about this. Coach the client to slow down, concentrate, and breathe deeply. You can recommend books and courses that teach breathing techniques.

Facilitating proper breathing patterns is a simple, incredibly effective method of interrupting anxiety. Listen for the slowing of breathing and remind clients to apply the easy techniques of slow, deep methodical breathing. Sometimes it is helpful for clients to close their eyes when following the instruction to breathe with the diaphragm. I tend to use this technique only to reestablish a sense of safety. I have also encouraged clients to pay closer attention to their own breathing, noticing when and where it becomes shallow in the world outside. Simply tracking breathing patterns can yield very interesting connections. Many sexual abuse survivors will note that their breathing becomes very shallow as soon as they turn off the lights. Others discover the pattern shifts after a specific set of auditory or visual triggers.

Mastery of breathing can be a powerful intervention. Breathing alone will not fix what hurts, but it is the single most powerful method of stopping panic or anxiety. Also, it is not addictive. One final suggestion: I sometimes ask clients to make a breathing bracelet as an art project. It simply serves as a reminder for clients to pay attention to and modify breathing patterns when necessary.

Grounding

Grounding techniques are simple and numerous. Clients in the midst of a triggering event or panic episode will often respond well to reminders of where they are. For example, during a flashback—one of the most dramatic aspects of a dissociative episode—clients lose track of time, place, and sometimes person. The clinician can often interrupt these episodes by asking, "Where are we? What is today's date?" In some instances, changing the setting, leaving the office, going for a brief walk, or getting the client a cup of coffee helps.

Minor interruptions in flow help reestablish a sense of safety. Occasionally I have asked clients to pick up the newspaper and read the date (however, this can backfire if the day's headlines are profoundly upsetting). I also ask clients to use the personal tools that they have derived to help remind them that they are in the here and now and safe. It is wise to have grounding tools prepared in advance with the input of the client. Have the client make a list and carry it in a wallet or purse. This can include the picture of a safe, supportive loved one; a picture of a pet; a safe or luck object or touchstone; or a prewritten message from the grounded self to the fearful self. Instruct the client to retrieve one or more of these tools if the regression occurs during a session. Most important, equipping your clients with grounding tools prepares them for triggering events outside the clinical setting. Under no circumstance endorse or empower any grounding technique that inflicts pain or hurts clients.

Thought-Stopping

Thought-stopping is part of a cognitive-behavioral tradition. The clinician works with the client in advance to derive a specific tool to stop an upsetting or compulsive thought. In its earliest form, the technique involved the use of rubber bands worn on the wrist that the client would snap to remind himself or herself that the thought needed to stop. Using rubber bands with trauma-related conditions is contraindicated since it can be zealously overused and instead of providing comfort, it can inflict pain. Instead, use benign interventions, such as the recitation of a saying or a nondenominational prayer, as a thought-stopping anchor. Never impose your saying or prayer on clients, especially with clients in early recovery. Some clients are adversely affected by even the most benign prayer. This includes, but is not limited to, survivors of religious abuse and/or ritual abuse. You can tell them what you favor or simply ask them to derive their own. Remember, impaired clients are hypersensitive and pseudocompliant. If you tell them something they do not like, your credibility may be diminished. Thought-stopping directives and objects must be benign and preferably derived by the client.

Declaration of Safety

Informed consent needs elaboration for clients with trauma-based disturbances. I tend to say something along the following lines: "I know this is a difficult process, and you may feel unsafe at times. This is normal. I will do all that I can to earn and maintain your trust. If I ever do anything that gives you a sense of nonsafety, please let me know. Sometimes something benign or unintended may result in discomfort. For example, a gesture, like raising an eyebrow, might make you uncomfortable. Please let me know at any time if anything that I say or do sets off a fear response. We are going to proceed at a pace that will not be overwhelming. We need to go at your pace, not mine.

We can also interrupt a session or talk about the weather if you get overloaded. We will accomplish what we strive for, but we must be sure that you feel safe. I also know that you will not trust me just because I say these things. Trust is earned, and I suspect you will need to test me. That is fine. We will learn together what you need. It is a process, and we will work carefully, slowly, and methodically. Now, do you have any comments or questions?"

A declaration of safety alone will not make you trustworthy. However, by putting into words your intention, that the therapy room will be a safe harbor, considerable relief may be afforded by your simply anticipating the client's fear of the process.

If I observe the client is still uncomfortable after my declaration of safety, I tend to add the following, "I know you have been told one thing and other things have happened. Violation of trust and the difference between words and actions are common aspects of what has injured so many people. I did not intend to add to your distrust by making a declaration of safety. I was simply stating my intent, and you will make your own judgments as we go forward. I only ask that you assist by letting me know when I do anything that increases your anxiety."

I recommend that clinicians compose their own declaration of safety tailored to the needs of specific clients.

Stop, Think, and Take Action

This concept was derived from military tradition. It is actually a cognitive-behavioral technique. I believe this concept started with the British Royal Navy, but I suspect its roots are far deeper. When a navy ship was attacked, chaos often ensued. Sailors would tend to freeze, run, or simply fail to remember standing orders. The Royal Navy trained the sailors to remember that when chaos surrounds you, you must stop what you are doing, evaluate (think), derive a course of action, and then put that plan into action. This is a very simple way of not succumbing to pure instinct. Instead, you are putting your brain back in charge.

I suggest that clients practice this technique and talk about when they have used it and how effective it was. Discuss in advance what actions would be appropriate, such as going for a walk, interrupting the flow, changing the channel, or ending a conversation. Most of the action involves disruption of an activity or circumstance that no longer feels safe. This principle is not set forth as a panacea; it is just one of many tools. One inherent advantage is that it clearly encourages the higher brain to make determinations of safety-enhancing action.

Avoiding Overstimulation

It is helpful to advise clients to avoid activities that might exacerbate anxiety. Now this may sound simple, but sometimes it is not so obvious. For example, I had a client who had trouble falling asleep. She had tried every technique the treatment team could think of. She cut out caffeine, reduced sugar, practiced breathing, exercised, and used non-addictive medication. Still, she had regular panic episodes in the evening, and like so many trauma clients, she either could not fall asleep or woke up with nightmares. I asked her what she did before going to bed, and she gave me considerable detail: She would get into bed and read some relaxing material, hoping to get tired. I asked her what she read that she considered relaxing. Her reply: "Stephen King, Dean Koonz, and Anne Rice novels." Simply asking her to change the reading list ameliorated the symptom. It is also interesting to note that this client was an attorney with an IQ that was off the charts, but she simply did not make the connection between the nightmarish books she read and the trouble she had getting to sleep. This may be part of the repetitive self-invalidation pattern so often seen in addicts with CPTSD.

Consider asking clients to avoid watching the news before going to bed. In some instances, it may be necessary for clients to avoid reading or watching the news completely until more stability is established. It is also necessary to comment on provocative dress or new activities that will result in intensity that will spill over. New relationships are most often discouraged, and this is completely congruent with early addiction recovery tradition.

Obsessive-Compulsive Displacement

Ruminative thinking, whether conscious or unconscious, is typical among trauma-based survivors. The most severely distressed will automatically assess a room for key features, including exits, placement of items, and number of blemishes on the walls or ceilings. Some clients will become distressed if a paper clip has been moved in their environment, and this sometimes will carry over to your office.

In addition to medication, displacement can be very helpful with the obsessive-compulsive features. By displacement, I mean purposely engaging in an obsessive task that is benign and often relaxing. Instead of soothing with food or chemicals, many clients feel relaxed when they do jigsaw puzzles, crossword puzzles, or play computer games such as solitaire or mahjongg. This technique can be a very potent method of self-soothing.

Self-Soothing

Self-soothing involves a wide range of possible techniques, as varied as each client's preferences. I prefer to derive these self-soothing activities individually with the client rather than impose an a priori list. Some fairly standard methods can include taking a warm, relaxing bath; recalling a soothing memory; visualizing a safe place; breathing; playing nonprovocative music; reading a children's book; hugging a stuffed animal; cuddling with a pet; walking the dog; calling a sponsor; reciting affirmations; and even rocking, which can also qualify as an OCD displacement. Although it looks frighteningly regressive, rocking is a good transitional tool for very distressed individuals. I usually advocate diminished use of rocking as the client builds strength.

Transitional Objects

Transitional objects are objects imbued with special meaning in accordance with neoanalytic theory, particularly object relations theory. According to this theory, infants have a complete dependence upon the mothering source. Once the mother leaves the room, the infant becomes terrified. In order to soothe the infant when she is not there, the mother will give the child an object—a blanket, toy, or pacifier—that serves as a mother substitute; or the infant may discover one on his or her own.

The clinician can decide with the client what might serve as a good transitional object. Stuffed animals are most frequently chosen. However, coins, pens, rings, jewelry, and other objects can work with equal efficacy. What matters is that the object is imbued with this special quality. A defined transitional object can be remarkably effective. In fact, AA coins and key chains appear to fit this description. It is also possible that rosaries or worry beads were derived as either transitional objects or displacement tools for obsessive behaviors. I am disinclined to suggest traditional religious symbols especially before the full range of the client's story and perception is known.

The question arises as to whether the clinician should suggest or gift the transitional object. I tend to favor the former over the latter, since it does not introduce confusing transference dynamics too early in the therapeutic process. Clinical boundary questions are further discussed in chapter 8.

Affirmations

Affirmations are a potent technique that was oversold in the 1980s and mercilessly mocked by comedians. However, affirmations or declarative self-statements have the potential of overriding the negative sublingual messages that seem to influence survivors. No, I am not trying to sound mystical, but survivors engage in a lot of fear-based inner dialogue, much of which is hostile, self-condemning, and fuel for feelings of hopelessness. Some of these voices, including the relapse voice, which operates on a slightly different channel, tell clients that they do not deserve for things to go well. They can never be forgiven. Affirmations, which are best derived individually, are intended to override these cognitions. Affirmations are also cognitive-behavioral tools. They are best recited aloud or in front of a mirror.

Many clients resist writing down affirmations, let alone reciting them. I may ask clients to tell me at least one positive affirmation during a session; many cannot do this. I then ask clients to simply write three to five personal positive affirmations. They are asked to repeat them during the next session and then instructed to read them at least twice daily. Subsequently, I ask them to say the affirmations aloud. Finally, they are asked to look in the mirror and recite them at least twice daily. David Barlow, an anxiety disorders specialist at Boston University, found that anxiety episodes can be triggered by simply looking in the mirror. Therefore, reciting affirmations in front of the mirror can at first be daunting, which is why I prefer to methodically work toward this goal. Properly used as part of the treatment protocol, affirmations can be an enormously effective tool.

Journaling

Journaling is another simple technique that can be helpful in a number of ways. More than simply a way of connecting feelings, journaling becomes part of a self-monitoring and self-empowering process. I ask clients to keep a journal of significant events so that they can become more objective and accurate observers of their emotional and cognitive states.

Journaling is not intended as a tool to retrieve memory. In fact, I ask that clients write a minimum of one sentence and a maximum of one page daily. I usually tell them, "We are not looking for a Hollywood narrative or the next articulate work of self-expression. We are simply looking for you to learn to observe with greater clarity what sets off your fear and what helps interrupt it. You need not be eloquent. We are not looking for profound insights, just simple trends and a journal of events to assist you with skill mastery. Some symptoms may go away simply by monitoring and recording them."

Journaling is a pivotal tool in learning to self-observe. In fact, I see it as a first step in becoming what cognitive-behavioral theorists describe as "becoming a self-scientist." This may sound cold and clinical at first, but it is truly part of the core clinical goal. We are seeking to educate and empower. Teaching clients key skills of self-management is vital. Journaling is part of that journey.

Attending Twelve Step Meetings

When triggered, clients tend to isolate. Similar to shallow breathing, isolation is an automatic response that adds to one's anxiety and sense of distress. In addition, triggered clients are likely to have relapse thoughts and cravings. Remember, the limbic system is fighting for control. Reminding the client to go to a meeting may help override the instinct to isolate, in addition to fighting the limbic urge to escape, use, and/or isolate.

Clearly, meetings can be helpful if clients are familiar with specific meetings and know some of the attendees and the likely themes. You may want to prepare clients by telling them that attending the meeting may seem difficult, but it is likely the right thing to do. It is okay if all they do at the meeting is listen. The meeting may or may not directly soothe. On some occasions, it can add to triggering or uniqueness perceptions. Anticipating this in advance, yet empowering the likely reality it will help more than hurt, assists the client in terms of realistic expectation from a specific meeting or home group.

Remind the client that the meeting is focusing on addiction, not necessarily the emotional trigger issue that caused acute discomfort. However, there is a strong possibility that one of the other attendees will be struggling with something that is similar. You might wish to say something like, "You must be around other people. I know your trust levels may be slightly impaired, but remember you trusted most of the people there before you were triggered. Keep good boundaries, stay safe, but go." You might wish to add, "Know the limitations of the individuals and group, so you don't use the situation to add to lack of trust in others. The benefits outweigh the risks. Check in with your sponsor. He or she is not your therapist, but is your advocate. So call your sponsor, attend meetings, and avoid the temptation to isolate."

Remember, the interpersonal dimension is one of the key dimensions. Going to meetings is not going to fix what hurts, but it can override the urge to isolate.

Reframing and Normalizing

With or without cognitive-behavioral training, almost all clinicians reframe information. Reframing, most simply stated, involves the articulation of a new perspective on a belief or cognition that often has a strong emotional foundation. The clinician challenges core beliefs and offers a new interpretation or framework for the client to see.

To some extent, primary addiction treatment involves a huge reframing of beliefs about substance use. From an "I"-centered perspective, the client is asked to look at addiction as a disease, not a problem of volitional control. I realize this is a massive oversimplification of the treatment process. In fact, I occasionally provide a client lecture interpreting the process of change in addiction treatment from the psychological perspective. The interpretation actually mirrors the Serenity Prayer, which can be construed as a reframing declarative.

Without belaboring the point, most clinicians use reframing all the time. The only addition I am making is that for trauma-related disorders, it is very helpful to use the first definition of PTSD as stated in chapter 2; that is, PTSD is a normal response to abnormal events. This permits a shift away from personal attribution, self-blame, and self-loathing. It effects a shift in cognition, which is what reframing is all about. On a larger scale, massive reframing based on evolution of thought, theoretical declaration, or most often solid science is called a zeitgeist.

Normalizing is also related to the first definition of PTSD. Clients with trauma-related disorders tend to think of themselves as uniquely bad, responsible, and loathsome. They enter therapy believing "I am the only one with these weird symptoms, thoughts, and feelings." The clinician can reassure clients that their symptoms fit within the parameters of the symptoms of other people. Conservative thinkers might see this as providing excuses. Not at all. Normalizing does not contradict personal responsibility, nor does it validate improper behavior. Normalizing is intended to soothe and disabuse the client from narcissistic overinterpretation that includes blaming and shaming oneself. Keep in mind that many survivors secretly fear they are crazy. In fact, dissociative episodes, fugue state, flashbacks, and cognitive intrusions do one heck of a good job in reinforcing these fears. So, learn the definitions, print them out, give them to clients, and repeat them. In my opinion, normalizing and distributing information about symptoms is good clinical practice.

"It's Not You; It's Your Addiction Speaking"

This phrase is a brilliant reframing used regularly by addiction professionals. It permits direct feedback or confrontation about behaviors or attitudes in a way that is not personal and reduces perceived threat. Applied to a triggered survivor or addict acting like a victim, the phrase is off target. This powerful phrase needs linguistic changes. Here are some examples I tend to use instead:

- "It seems to me that you might be engaging in victim behavior."
- "It seems like your limbic system has hijacked your rational self (or higher thinking)."
- "You seem to be 'going limbic.'"
- "It seems like without knowing it, you might have switched back into a mode where compulsive and repetitive self-invalidation is in progress."
- "It's not you; it is a triggering event."

Using the right words will help validate, soothe, and reframe. Reframing is a variation of something called a Ginotian intervention, the essence of which is "It's not you; it's the behavior."

Martial Arts

The use of martial arts is a powerful adjunct, not simply a technique. It is most often appropriately included after you have established a good therapeutic alliance, certainly not in the first session. Martial arts provide skills of empowerment and a sense of mastery.

The martial arts are not for everyone but can be a tremendous source of discipline and redirected intensity. Not for getting even, martial arts can be seen as part of the self-empowerment that will protect the client going forward. It can also provide an aerobic outlet. Which martial art to pursue is mostly up to the client. I tend to favor the more defensive options, particularly tai chi, which involves slow, methodical moving, tremendous concentration, and a fitness and health maintenance emphasis.

Meditation, Guided Imagery, and Relaxation Training

A plethora of tapes, books, and workbooks are available to teach these techniques. Whereas some clinicians use them as the centerpiece of therapy, I usually assign meditation, guided imagery, or relaxation as part of what goes on in a residential program or at home between sessions.

Some tools are specifically designed with instructions for trauma survivors; they may or may not be better for your client than a more generic version. The bottom line is that you want your client to begin practicing these techniques. These methods require repetition and practice. I tell my clients that as their relaxation and meditation abilities improve, and as they work through therapy in building more strength, the likelihood of unmanageable triggers substantially decreases over time. This sets a more realistic expectation of progress, not perfection or instant mastery.

Imagery is powerful and can be used as a stabilizing tool. In terms of guided imagery, I recommend careful selection. Some older tools have an agenda involving memory retrieval. Others may include instructions or imagery that might not match your client's needs or serve as triggers.

Reflective Listening and Mirroring

Every clinician knows about reflective listening, one of the core skills in building a therapeutic alliance. Reflective listening is a necessary skill or technique that helps reassure the client. For clients with trauma-based disorders, there is one caveat. Do not say, "I understand." The reason I recommend avoiding this wording is quite simple: Unless you were there, in precisely the traumatic circumstances the client went through, you can't understand. To make the claim of understanding runs the risk of invalidation.

Instead of using the generic Rogerian comment of "I understand," I tend to specifically correct myself or simply say, "I comprehend, but obviously I can never fully understand." This extra measure shows a profound respect for the sanctity of the client's experience of the event. Whereas we seek to normalize and battle "uniqueness," it is important to honor the unique aspect of the client's personal experience. This extra step may seem like a simple semantic exercise, but it really helps the client know that you respect his or her individual emotional state and are not glibly claiming to understand something you have not experienced.

This principle still applies even if you have been through similar circumstances. Keep in mind that an individual perceives each event, and proclamations even from a fellow survivor can be invalidating. I observed that Vietnam vets from different branches of service, or different times in service, had very unique experiences and perceptions. My own experience with chemotherapy taught me that there are common factors, but each individual has his or her own idiosyncratic journey with different levels of reactivity and sensitivity.

So, watch the language and be aware of the individuality of the listener. Simple phrases of reassurance, such as "I know how you feel" or "I know what you've been through," can have negative effects.

Hugging and Other Touching Gestures

Standards for mental health professionals are quite clear: Hugging a client is not sanctioned, recommended, or appropriate. You do not touch the client, except perhaps for a handshake. In the addiction treatment world, hugging is more accepted. It is most often benign and simply part of the greeting or departure tradition consistent with meetings. Do not assume that a survivor will want or interpret even a routine gesture or greeting ritual, such as a hug, without feeling compromised. However, when a session terminates and there is a clear need or the client makes the request, it may become appropriate. Again, I would prefer to administer a pat to the shoulder as opposed to the hug, but instinct, training, and circumstance will ultimately guide you.

If you perceive a strong need for a hug or other gesture from the client, do not simply act without asking for permission. The gesture can easily be misinterpreted, especially if the client was extremely emotional during the session. If after a particularly painful session your clinical instincts say the client needs some support, it is preferable to use words. I might say something like, "This was a very intense session for you. I have every confidence that the intensity will pass, perhaps not immediately. I encourage you to apply some of the techniques we discussed to help you with grounding. We talked about your personal toolbox, so rely on it and try to add to it. Therapy is not always this painful or intense. If things are really difficult, we may need to meet more often until things settle down. I will leave that judgment to you."

I can think of no circumstance for the clinician, without very specific training and supervision, where any other form of touching is indicated. Despite technique trends suggesting we can make greater, quicker breakthroughs by using physical interventions involving touch, I strongly suggest that touching not be part of formal therapy. Always stay within your training and expertise. For the most part, the majority of clinicians use verbal interventions and techniques. Do not stray from the basics of conservative training. You can display empathy completely with words. Empathy and support are tempting to administer, but there is little evidence to support the notion that in isolation, direct or physical displays of empathy improve outcome. Certainly, having compassion, and communicating it conservatively, is part of the therapeutic alliance. Do stay within strict boundaries, especially with addicted trauma-disorder clients.

Using Humor

A sense of humor can be an invaluable technique or tool in assisting clients with trauma-based disorders. Be careful with humor since we are dealing with a hypersensitive population. By the same token, the hypersensitivity can be partially ameliorated with tasteful ironic or humorous comments. For example, one client was late for a session, and she kept saying, "I'm sorry." The next several sessions she kept apologizing. So, I began a short-term ritual of greeting her with the nickname "I'm Sorry." She laughed, and I intermittently would repeat the greeting.

Similarly, another difficult and extremely depressed client had alienated all of her peers. I asked her why, and she said, "Because I am frumpy and grumpy." "Frumpy and Grumpy" became her nickname, and the humor helped diffuse the pain and modify her conduct. I use it with great caution but remarkable success. I try to compliment clients with humor, using irony as a means of getting past their "damned if you do, damned if you don't" attitude. So, if a client is doing well, I will administer the compliment packaged in irony. I might say: "You are doing pretty well considering you are so grumpy, frumpy, and impossible to please." Such paradoxical compliments can be a stealthy and effective means of building ego-strength.

Writing a Mission Statement

Therapy is a very complex process, but defining the overall goal can be remarkably easy. One technique I regularly employ early in the process is to ask the client to write the equivalent of a mission statement. Corporations do this to define what they do and what they represent. Trauma-based clients who are often clueless and lack clear direction benefit from this exercise. Asking clients to write their mission statement in a paragraph or two can be revealing. The statements can help the clinician understand the client's goals and how realistic they are. The mission statement serves as a simple and effective self-declaration of a personal goal that can be later modified by the clinician and client.

Containment

One of the unstated aspects of therapy is helping clients contain the flood of feelings and memories of a traumatic event. To some extent, clinicians are containers. We listen with compassion, yet we remain calm as role models of containment. This is why it is essential for clinicians to remain composed, rational, and professional, no matter what we hear. Getting emotional for or with clients is countertherapeutic.

We can also articulate the goal of containment. This fits in terms of teaching specific skills. I tend to openly advocate improving containment skills, not denial or dissociation skills, as part of the healing process.

Some of the techniques already discussed are congruent with the clinical objective of containment. I view containment as a first step toward acceptance, or earlier in the therapy process, I avoid the word "acceptance" and instead use terms like "co-existing with the pain" or "moving toward a ceasefire in your internal civil war."

Displacement

Displacement, the technique of substituting one form of intensity for another, can, if carefully selected, have some salutary effect. Displacement should never be destructive. Instead, displacement techniques should build confidence or strength. For example, some clients get some relief from anger, fear, or intense emotion by doing push-ups or squeezing a grip-strengthening ball. Some feel better going for a run or using the treadmill or other exercise equipment.

If used as a temporary technique, and if there are limits in terms of not inflicting self-pain, strength-building displacement techniques can be helpful in the short-term. Do carefully monitor the client. Be careful that clients do not use these techniques in an addictive manner. Addicts are at risk for becoming compulsive, so good judgment is warranted. Clients with a history of compulsive behaviors are at very high risk for misusing displacement techniques. For example, some eating-disorder clients have a history of compulsive exercising, so exercise is not recommended.

I tend to prefer rapid movement away from displacement and encourage the more comprehensive goals around "sublimation" or pro-social activity as a means of redirecting intensity. An addict with trauma issues may become a runner, but rather than endorsing this outlet only, I might encourage him or her to do volunteer work at a foodshelf, train therapy dogs, or participate in fund-raisers for abused children. Encouraging displacement activities that have more meaning tend to be more effective than simple displacement techniques. Purpose-driven displacements, those that involve meaningful activities, are the same as teleological interventions.

Ice Bucket and Red Marker Techniques

For clients intent on feeling pain, these unconventional and rarely used techniques may, under unusual circumstances, have some short-term utility. For example, if a client is cutting himself or herself and seems obsessed with inflicting pain, the ice bucket technique can be a safe alternative. Essentially, if a client feels like cutting, the client immerses his or her arm in ice water instead. This is indeed painful, especially after a minute or two. In theory it is not harmful, but if the client has an underlying medical condition, this technique can seriously backfire. Never use this technique without medical clearance and close supervision. The technique is mostly intended for inpatient use. Personally, I have never used this, nor do I recommend it.

The red marker technique is another intervention intended to interrupt self-cutting. Rather than actual cutting, the client uses a Magic Marker, usually with indelible ink, to mark rather than cut. This may interrupt the cutting ritual and facilitate thought rather than impulse. In theory, the client can see what he or she would have done and has time to discuss it with the therapist and/or peers. Again, I have never used this technique.

Expressive Techniques

Many techniques are based on the belief that expressing repressed emotion will ultimately be therapeutic. In certain instances, expressive techniques are necessary and appropriate components of a balanced, integrative therapeutic approach. However, when applied too zealously or with the wrong clients, expressive techniques can cause considerable harm.

Psychodrama and Gestalt Techniques

Psychodrama is a group technique that encourages clients to express repressed emotions with the help of the group. Some clinicians are very skilled with this technique, and the scenarios with trauma clients can be extremely intense. Too often, due to its intensity, this technique gives the illusion of breaking through. On the basis of my experience, psychodrama tends to do far more harm than good. Psychodrama dramatically "opens up" people, but this is not really the goal in trauma-related therapy. We may want some intensity, but not drama without context, closure, and a larger therapeutic goal.

Gestalt techniques, including open chair techniques, are also not productive with this population.

Creating a Time Line

This technique can be helpful, if applied at the proper time. Used prematurely, it can trigger your client and set off a nonproductive, obsessional quest for more detail and a reliving of the past. Properly timed, however, in either a group or individual setting, this technique can help connect emotions and permit an objective history-tracking tool.

Looking at the sequence of events written on a piece of paper helps in terms of framing. It provides a cognitive perspective of events as real, objectively delineated, and connected. The technique can bring back intense feelings. Individual debriefing and extra therapy time may be necessary when this technique is utilized. Just as addicts make breakthroughs doing addiction time lines or calculating the cost of the addiction, the exercise of drawing a time line is a powerful intervention for trauma clients, requiring careful timing.

Telling One's Story

Most addiction clients tell their story rather early in recovery. I tend to advocate that trauma clients focus their chemical use story on their using history and not articulate their abuse or trauma history at the same time. I encourage clients to separate the two tasks and skim over the trauma part until the timing is in their favor. For clients, telling their addiction story is stressful enough without adding their story of trauma. Sorting out highly emotional and traumatic pieces isn't easy. However, it is a good idea to remind clients that the main task of telling their story in an addiction therapy group or Twelve Step meeting is intended to focus primarily on the development of the disease of addiction. The challenge of telling one's story in terms of trauma, say in a trauma group for example, can be quite daunting, therapeutic, or possibly countertherapeutic. It is all about timing.

Not all clients need group therapy to heal from trauma. Group tends to accelerate healing but can overwhelm some. Some clinicians use the time line technique to prepare the telling of one's story. Telling one's story in a group setting can help in terms of acceptance, distance, objectivity, and reframing. Telling and hearing similar stories can be immensely therapeutic. Knowing there are others who feel what they feel is soothing. This is the core of Yalom's (1995) universality principle of group dynamics. However, some clients may become flooded or obsessed with a memory quest or feel more negative.

Telling one's story is a powerful intervention and must be used cautiously. I see the main objective as an exercise of gaining mastery over history and limbic intrusion and reinforcing containment skills.

God Box

This technique involves clients writing down their resentments and ritually placing them in their Higher Power's hands. Appropriately timed, this can be an effective technique to "let go and let God."

A less effective variant of this technique involves clients writing down their resentments, emotions, recollection, or pain and then burying or burning the paper. In my opinion, this second example feeds the illusion of "getting rid of it," which is really not a realistic goal. In reality, we are moving clients toward acceptance and coexistence with the pain and the history, and the notion of letting go is a far more effective goal.

Letter Writing

Letter writing is more than an expressive tool. I do not encourage angry, emotional outpouring. At first, I may encourage the client to write an unedited letter to the perpetrator, using whatever language expresses the feeling. I then ask the client to put the letter aside and revisit it a week later. When appropriate I will ask the client to rewrite the letter in the most assertive and balanced way he or she can.

The goal of the second writing, which is more difficult than the first, is to link emotions and words in a balanced statement without rage or terror. The larger objective is making peace with one's self, not necessarily forgiving the perpetrator. Letter writing is an effective tool that facilitates assertiveness, strength building, and balance.

Scream Techniques and Reliving the Trauma

The peak of popularity for the scream technique was the Janov scream therapy of the 1970s. Simply stated, it is not an effective technique. In fact, screaming and reenactment of anger seem to facilitate holding on, not letting go. The transitory relief felt by clients who scream, punch pillows, or break objects is often followed by angry obsession and an endless reliance on expression that never really fulfills the hoped-for purpose. Behavioral evidence suggests these techniques facilitate holding on to anger and reinforce fantasy, obsession, or acting-out.

Some clients have a strong urge to relive their traumatic event. For example, one of my clients said, "I just want to go out, get raped, and punch the guy in the mouth." Obviously, this urge is not healthy and just like chemical relapse must be discouraged. The notion of reliving the event with words during a session resides on a difficult boundary. Whereas "bringing fear into the room" is desirable, we do not want actions or behaviors that reinforce intense reliving in a quest for changed outcome. This chaos-seeking and attempt to change history are countertherapeutic. So, too, is being immersed in memory or fantasy rehearsal. In general, I do not suggest the use of a technique that might add to the client's quest for chaos or perfect outcome.

We do need some intensity in the clinical realm, but timing, intensity, and purpose are vital decision points. Be conservative. More distressed clients want to push for more intensity when it is not in their best interest. This is where sound clinical judgment is essential. In general, be conservative. If in doubt, confer with a colleague or clinician with trauma expertise. Half of life might be timing, but more than half of therapy depends upon proper timing.

Controlled Evocative Exposure

This technique is part of a woven strategy where exposure is not the main emphasis. Instead, the clinical goals incorporate a wider process, not just symptom management. Clients in group or individual therapy may intellectualize too much or, more accurately, may be so dissociative or detached that the process has little impact. The goal is not to "flood," but to add a modicum of intensity. As traditional theory argues, change is best effected during a crisis. Certainly we do not want to engineer a crisis, but at times a bit of intended intensity can be helpful. It is certainly *inadvisable* to put a very fragile client in most group processes.

Controlled evocative exposure incorporates very conservative use of exercise or stimuli that elicit a mild response, one that enhances but does not overstimulate. My favorite controlled evocative technique is the use of movies, especially in a group setting. In my work with Vietnam vets, we used a specific list of movies and showed them at specific times during treatment. Similarly, at my current treatment center, I provide a lecture to the group and show a movie, such as *Fearless,* then use it as a tool for discussion. What is interesting is that all but the most fragile clients—who should not yet be in a group in the first place—find it empowering to see an actor portray themes, behaviors, attitudes, and contradictions that are part of trauma-based phenomena. They not only identify; they become more objective and rational about their condition. It does demystify, and in the process of a group of survivors discussing the dynamics and linking personal experience, the group members are moved further along the continuum of acceptance and mastery.

Finally, "putting it up on the screen" is part of what visual kinesthetic dissociation (VKD), a power technique, advocates. I also put it in terms of developing a stronger observer superego as protector, guide, or coach. The development of an observer superego is not endorsing a dissociative identity disorder (DID) "protector persona." Instead, it involves healthy differentiation, perhaps dissociative in nature, but it really reinforces higher cognition over limbic control. The "observer" is an enhancement, a sort of officer meant to protect from harm by using objectivity and rationality, not exercising control but containment.

Other tools can be employed, including some conservative writing assignments and even role play. The key is to keep these tools instructive, controlled, and conservative. The goal is to generate just enough intensity so as to enhance mastery and learning. Doing this in a group setting helps in terms of "universality," a term Yalom coined and is now part of the clinical lexicon.

Use of Hallucinogens

I included the use of hallucinogens under expressive techniques, even though it really is part of a very peculiar category. Bad ideas take a long time to die, especially if there is a scintilla of validity, taken out of context. In the search for a cure for PTSD, chemicals have been employed. We had pentathol and other barbiturates used in the front lines of World War II. Indeed, pentathol appeared to work so well, permitting the soldier to "safely" relive the trauma, that it became standard fare in many movies and television shows. In reality, the method was abandoned. It was not effective and rather dangerous. However, the quest for a chemical tool for therapy continued in other venues.

The use of LSD to treat alcoholism was popular for quite some time until it failed to show merit and caused damage. The Central Intelligence Agency (CIA) tried LSD in the now infamous subway experiments. Perhaps Timothy Leary contributed most to the death of therapeutic LSD but propelled it into recreational popularity with ongoing damaging and at times devastating consequences. Recently, the use of chemicals to facilitate expression has reemerged.

Use of Ecstasy

Ecstasy (MDMA) is a stimulant and a hallucinogen advocated by some clinicians as a treatment for PTSD. Ecstasy rapidly produces an excess of serotonin, creating an intense sense of well-being. It also has hallucinogenic features. Thus, it creates an altered state, pleasant for most, and strong enough to change boundaries and rationality. Proponents claim that it permits recall and recitation of trauma without the panic or fear. Some claim that you can program hypnotic suggestions, such as "The trauma is over and all will be okay now."

Ecstasy, originally called Empathy, was used to treat couples having intimacy problems. When it became a street drug and reemerged as Ecstasy, its use as a therapeutic agent was prohibited. In 2002, Ecstasy promoters successfully petitioned the Food and Drug Administration (FDA) claiming this "therapeutic" tool merits further investigation. I do not comprehend the legal arguments but the Ecstasy advocates won, and they have a research project planned. The advocates claim that the dose will be carefully controlled and no harm will be done. I suspect the initial results will show it works. Indeed, almost any induced altered state will help in some way. An altered state can be life-changing and as we know there is a downside as well: A bad trip can be terrifying. Additionally, the altered state stimulates addiction. Suddenly, we have addiction, cross addiction, and likely brain damage. This "research" will likely encourage more to use this damaging chemical in a recreational fashion. Additional casualties are an almost certainty.

Use of Ibogain

Ibogain has been recently touted as a PTSD cure. The hallucinogenic agent is a South African root, used by indigenous shamans, that induces an altered state. It is also being used offshore by an enthusiastic American researcher as a tool to treat chronic relapse and PTSD. The mass media described Ibogain as a powerful new possibility. Fortunately, Ibogain has not gained acceptance, despite considerable press exposure. Several years ago I treated a chronically relapsing alcoholic who had received Ibogain therapy. He was indeed abstemious, but his underlying bipolar disorder, likely fueled by Ibogain, led him to believe he was God's agent. He was sober, actually attended AA meetings, but compulsively sought females with whom he could share his divine mysticism.

■

In this chapter, we have reviewed a wide variety of techniques applicable to clients with trauma disorders. Some techniques are simple, yet elegant. Some techniques are oriented toward containment, and others are oriented toward expression. Some are dangerous and irrational. The list is only partial but does reflect the confusing set of options available. Today's clinician needs many tools to work with today's complex clients. How these tools are woven together is part of a personal crafting that cannot be easily summarized or taught.

■ ■ ■

CHAPTER SIX

THERAPEUTIC MODELS, POWER TECHNIQUES, TELEOLOGY, AND PROCESS

The delineation between technique and therapeutic model is difficult and somewhat arbitrary. Chapter 5 reviewed a variety of techniques that can be used within a particular model or included as part of several models. Chapter 5 also included comments on expressive techniques. Gestalt and psychodrama techniques may be utilized as part of a more integrated and balanced framework, but caution is urged. I will not repeat my cautionary statements here, which are more applicable when a Gestalt, psychodrama, or similar therapeutic model is exclusively utilized.

Chapter 6 will review the larger framework: therapeutic models or more comprehensive systems of therapy. In addition, this chapter reviews power techniques, teleology, and process.

Power techniques are attractive models that can have a dramatic impact in treating trauma clients. Effective, but not mystical, these approaches can be part of an integrated method of treating clients with trauma disorders. I am including somatic therapies as a subset of power techniques, a somewhat arbitrary decision since somatic therapies are relatively new, yet connected to several older models.

Teleology, or the delineation of a clear future goal, is a new approach specifically geared toward complex survivors (those more likely to have co-occurring addictions).

Process refers to the overall synthesis of the therapy processes and is part of the clinician's art form, not necessarily connected to any particular technique or model.

These considerations are part of the foundation necessary to embrace an integrated picture, one that each clinician synthesizes. The variety of options should stimulate critical, informed, and independent thinking. All of this will prepare the reader for my recommendations and synthesis in chapter 8.

Therapy Models

A therapeutic model is defined as an organized system of thinking and delivering treatment. What follows is a short list of the many therapy models available to clinicians for treating trauma disorders.

Analytic Therapy and Neoanalytic Therapy

Analytic therapy and neoanalytic therapy are variations of traditional Freudian therapy. Predicated upon the general notion that traumatic events have interrupted developmental milestones, the clinician is encouraged to let the client derive insights during the therapeutic process. The client is encouraged to invest considerable time and effort in finding the missing pieces, uncovering the trauma, and letting go of fantasy.

Well-meaning, and rigorously articulated, this model has a rich literature, is brilliantly descriptive, but has essentially no scientific validation. The analytic process requires the clinician to be the central focal point for all issues. The clinician encounters significant intensity and must maintain complete neutrality. The main goal is to facilitate the client reaching his or her own insights, subsequently working through powerful emotional issues. Insight is the goal, and individual therapy is almost always the preferred means. Sadly, many clients become immersed in this method and larger issues can get lost, including the recognition of an addictive disorder.

Strict analytic practitioners tend to resist medication, preferring not to interfere with a pure therapeutic process. In addition, the clinician is discouraged from taking any directive role in guiding an often-desperate client. This approach takes years to complete. Most clients do not get better, and much of the literature describes transference and countertransference issues. It is upon this model that borderline dogma, the set of diagnostic and therapeutic assumptions, has been derived. This includes the damnation of being untreatable. Analytic thinking can be a helpful clinical resource, but in its pure and traditional form, complex survivors, particularly those with addictive disorders, are not likely to thrive.

Cognitive-Behavioral Therapy

Most readers are familiar with cognitive-behavioral approaches. Cognitive-behavioral therapy (CBT) involves behavioral goal-setting coupled with a respect and understanding that we are dealing with more than just mechanics. The recognition, validation, and connection made with the client are part of the process. The notion that people use thought as part of the determination of conduct, not merely conditioning protocols, is emphasized. As such, the internal dialogue is part of the model.

CBT techniques are varied and often involve formal goal-setting and some verbal or written contract delineation. The therapeutic alliance does not simply focus on insight or abreaction. Instead, clinician and client work together toward specific changes in behavior suggested by the clinician and endorsed by the client. The clinician teaches specific skills and suggests alternatives, options, or different cognitions.

Reframing is part of CBT, as are many fundamental techniques. Rehearsal of specific skills may occur during the session, and assignments between sessions are common. A key emphasis is upon building ego strength, modifying maladaptive behaviors, and challenging misguided or inaccurate beliefs. Thought-stopping is another technique that falls under the rubric of CBT.

CBT involves a wide range of options, tools, and techniques. I tend to see it as part of a synthesis. It takes the best of the behavioral tradition and operationalizes a plethora of techniques geared toward specific skill building and ego strengthening. The clinician works together with the client, seeking to specifically target symptoms and change behaviors and attitudes. CBT does not hide in mysticism, nor is it steeped in a process that waits for certain dynamics to be displayed. The clinician and the client work together toward improving quality of life.

Little wonder that CBT has the most research supporting its efficacy. In fact, *Effective Treatments for PTSD* (Foa, Keane, and Friedman 2000), the product of the Guidelines Task Force of the International Society for Traumatic Stress Studies, describes CBT as the most consistently effective and research-substantiated approach available. It is the gold standard approach by which other more elaborate techniques need to be compared.

Dialectical Behavior Therapy

Dialectical behavior therapy (DBT), an extension of cognitive-behavioral therapy, was created by Marsha Linehan and is wonderfully explicated in *Cognitive-Behavioral Treatment of Borderline Personality Disorder.*

DBT was developed as a year-long, highly structured program for persons with borderline personality disorder. Linehan developed the dialectical component following her own apparent exhaustion from working with this complex and challenging client population. She astutely blended Eastern thinking with the cognitive-behavioral tradition.

Linehan (1993) describes her model as a blend, or fusion. Linehan's model has rightly become a very popular framework. Some of the techniques articulated by Linehan blend empathy, firm limit setting, and accountability. One of the early clinical foci was to minimize "noise," that is, the disruptive, nonproductive, and chaos-generating behavior of people with borderline personality disorder. Another technique Linehan describes is the use of a gong to facilitate cognitive focus. DBT teaches self-control, impulse management, and appropriate behavior. It has been woven into outpatient service models as well as addiction treatment settings.

In my opinion, DBT is one of the best systems to come along in many years. Essentially, Linehan challenges the Western tradition of "either/or" thinking and normalizes contradiction. When contradiction is seen as "no big deal," the clinician is taking away some of the pathological sting from the phenomenon of "borderline splitting."

As discussed in chapter 2, the tendency for trauma survivors to become more "black and white" is normal. Clients who develop trauma-related disorders experience "ego fractionation," or the splitting of ego. This internal splitting, part of the phenomenon of dissociation, results in contradictory behavior. The dialectical model embraces and normalizes these contradictions. As such, it fosters acceptance and does not make a normal process feel pathological. Certainly, this is done in a highly gentle manner, not in a dismissive or confrontational fashion. Style, not just message, matters. This framework facilitates normalization of contradiction as well as acceptance of contradiction. Using the term "complex trauma survivor" instead of "borderline" and adding in Twelve Step work can enhance DBT techniques.

Exposure Therapy

Exposure therapies purposively and systematically expose clients to fear-inducing circumstances. Based upon the behavioral principle of successive approximation, the client gradually builds skill and mastery. The clinician does not put the client in the face of actual harm, but specific stimuli are methodically introduced. Eventually, the clinician might accompany the client to an anxiety-producing site and help him or her walk through it safely. The main goal is teaching skills of anxiety management.

Several variants of exposure therapy have been developed, including prolonged exposure therapy. There is no evidence to support one variation over the other, and some creative labeling builds an expectation of superiority before specific data can be assembled. Nonetheless, behavioral techniques, along with cognitive-behavioral techniques, have more of a research foundation than analytic models. It should be noted that exposure techniques are very similar to systematic desensitization and rational emotive therapy (RET).

Exposure therapy has become a major focal point for research-oriented clinicians, and there is convincing research that exposure therapy may yield very good results. It should be noted that exposure differs from flooding. The goal is not to overwhelm but to build mastery. In the hands of a well-trained clinician, exposure techniques have merit. However, for those without specific training, there is the risk of flooding rather than skill building. Therefore, I advise caution in the application of these techniques. In addition, exposure techniques do not incorporate the necessary breadth and scope needed for complex trauma survivors (those most likely to suffer from a co-occurring addiction).

Virtual Reality

Virtual reality methods are presently under development. The use of computer simulations may provide a powerful method of restimulating traumatic memories and, in a controlled setting, facilitate mastery. The technology holds promise in engineering specific cues, triggers, and feelings. For example, a person who has had a traumatic episode involving height might be able to experience a falling sensation in a controlled laboratory setting. In terms of skill building, this exposure, although intense, may facilitate the necessary mastery to utilize actual environmental cues.

Some clients are so overwhelmed by anticipatory anxiety that they cannot bridge the gap from office to real life. Virtual reality, when perfected and applied judiciously with a skilled clinician, may be able to help bridge the gap between practice and real life. As with exposure therapy, this method may not sufficiently address the needs of more complex clients.

Power Techniques

The passion surrounding power techniques has few parallels in the mental health world. The intensity of emotions many clinicians exhibit would suggest we are talking about religion, not treatment. I have heard clinicians declare, "I would never refer a client to a facility that uses eye movement desensitization and reprocessing (EMDR)." Conversely, another clinician would state, "I would never refer to a facility that didn't use EMDR." Indeed, a damned if you do, damned if you don't dynamic. Sounds like some of our more complex clients.

Eye Movement Desensitization and Reprocessing

Developed by Francine Shapiro, eye movement desensitization and reprocessing (EMDR) appeared in 1991. The goal of EMDR is to assist clients in mastering composure while recalling the details of a traumatic event. During the procedure, the client is instructed to indicate to the clinician if he or she is becoming overloaded by raising one, two, or three fingers, depending upon the perceived level of discomfort. The client is told that he or she can slow things down or stop if necessary. Clients are also told that they will be viewing or reviewing a traumatic episode as if they were riding on a train. This directive provides the distance and objectivity analogous to the observer superego discussed earlier. Other directions are read, and the parameters are systematically defined. The client is relaxed and focused and knows that he or she will be talking about painful memories. The clinician then asks the client to follow the rhythmic motion of the clinician's finger, or an object such as a pencil, while the painful memory is recited.

EMDR is repeated as the client builds more and more comfort and mastery. Additional memories are targeted; the term "node" is used to describe connected parts of memory. The expectation is that the recitation will be safe, and the client will be able to manage the emotion and memory without being overwhelmed.

Originally, EMDR was interpreted as visual gating. Some clinicians speculated that by activating the visual cortex, the brain better modulated the limbic system, thereby reactivating the gating function interrupted by the hippocampus being off-line. Research has now shown that the visual part, the eye movement, is not the operant variable. Auditory stimuli, alternately administered to one ear and then the other, are equally effective. Thus, it may be that distracting or multitasking reactivates the gating function.

The bottom line is that it works. Why, is not yet clear, but it does appear to be helpful. Whether it has anything more to offer than CBT or other techniques is not yet known. Several creative offshoots, using other stimuli, have been marketed. The debate continues but the technique is helpful and does not seem to do harm. It shares many common aspects of Ericksonian hypnosis as well as traditional desensitization models. Science will eventually sort out the effective ingredient(s).

Visual Kinesthetic Dissociation

Visual kinesthetic dissociation (VKD) was developed as part of neurolinguistic programming during the late 1970s. A mixture of classic hypnosis using Milton Erickson's approach and Erik Fromm's dissociation of ego technique, VKD is essentially an exposure technique teaching skills of detachment or dissociation.

VKD teaches clients to envision their body position (kinesthesia) during a traumatic event. The client is taught to detach himself or herself from the kinesthetic memory. The claim is that recalling a memory from a "decentered" perspective will facilitate a "visual kinesthetic reframe" of the experience.

Clients are taught several observation perspectives, borrowing heavily from Fromm's observer ego concept. Clients are asked to visualize themselves in a movie projection booth or behind a camera that can pull back or even leave the situation, if necessary. This learned dissociation encourages clients to envision their pre-trauma selves. Clients are also told that they can adjust the color, volume, and emotional intensity of a traumatic recollection. As emotions and memory become more stable, the clinician might ask the client to run the event backward. In essence, the client becomes reconditioned, learning to have a sense of detachment and perhaps even mastery. The therapist provides many empowering suggestions during the process, and the client is reinforced to feel safe in the here and now, anchored with the therapist.

Several creative variations of this technique have been developed. There are numerous explanations as to why the technique works, some esoteric, others fanciful. Some evidence shows it is effective, when properly applied and with the proper client. It is not a panacea and can facilitate setbacks if used with a highly fragile client.

Thought Field Therapy

Thought field therapy (TFT), sometimes known as the Callahan technique, was developed by Roger Callahan during the 1980s and has become more elaborate with time. A creative synthesis of Eastern constructs and Western "technology," TFT claims to work by tapping various parts of the body in order to rebalance natural energy systems. The tapping, done along acupuncture meridians, purportedly corrects "perturbations" in the energy field, called thought fields, correcting the disruption. Different algorithms or tapping sequences are used to treat different symptoms. A very specialized verbal algorithm, called voice technology, claims to extract key information from the human voice resulting in a reduction of the energy disturbance and a reduction of psychological distress.

Considered by many to be filled with hype and unproven claims, this technique is supported by little empirical evidence. However, some clients appear to improve. Whereas more study is needed, the formality of the technique, as well as its blend of Eastern energy theory and scientific-sounding techniques coupled with physical distraction, may help some clients. Some observers claim that TFT and EMDR are essentially the same, one using finger tapping and the other finger waving.

The Counting Method

Introduced by Frank Ochberg in 1988, the counting method is remarkably simple. After establishing a healthy therapeutic bond, the therapist asks the client to recall a traumatic memory while the therapist methodically counts to one hundred at a rate of one number per second in a steady, reassuring voice. The client is told that he or she should recall the event with increasing intensity as the clinician counts forward. Maximum intensity is to be at the number forty. After forty, the client should imagine leaving the past memory and coming to the present as the count reaches ninety. At ninety-three or ninety-four the therapist says, "Back to here," to guide the client back to the immediate moment.

The counting method works, theoretically, in several ways. First, the traumatic memory is connected to the therapist's voice and to the reassuring experience of the therapy. Whether this is conditioning or hypnosis can be debated. Second, the memory is contained and replayed in a brief interval, lasting less than two minutes. The therapist and client agree on this containment interval, and successful completion demonstrates potential mastery of what may have been overwhelming memory. Finally, the intensity of the memory is purposely raised and lowered during the counting. This further enhances a sense of mastery.

The counting method is consistent with EMDR, hypnosis, desensitization, and flooding. The exact mechanisms for this technique and other power techniques have not been scientifically established. Although there are testimonials, it is not yet known if the technique is effective and how it compares to the gold standard of cognitive-behavioral approaches. On a positive note, Ochberg does articulate the need to incorporate some aspects of meaning when dealing with trauma's consequences.

All of the power techniques discussed above have some factors in common. They appear to be derivatives of Gestalt-based techniques using variations of Ericksonian hypnosis, neurolinguistic programming, and distraction. They also seem to have charismatic founders who deeply believe in the technique, sometimes resulting in an almost cultlike following among clients and professionals. Whereas scientific analysis will be the ultimate arbiter, we cannot ignore methods, even if flawed, that appear to be doing something worthwhile.

I believe that the core component of these techniques involves two key factors: formal induction (expectancy) and multitasking (distraction). The expectancy effect is well documented. If we believe something will help, it likely will. The distraction component will have some connection in how we are wired in processing information and emotion. Visual, emotional, and traumatic information seem to take very different and apparently specific pathways. We are only beginning to unravel this complex design. I suspect that in a safe setting, the therapist is able to facilitate clients' "tapping into" several pathways at once. It is likely that the brain relearns or returns to its baseline state of greater integration.

Another notion is that the "gating" mechanisms are restored—specifically, the gating between the limbic system and the neocortex. I suspect with time, the actual mechanisms involved will have firm grounding in neuroanatomy and methodical research. In the interim, it is logical to use power techniques conservatively and judiciously as part of a larger plan for facilitating client integration, not simply symptom containment.

Finally, it should be noted that some master clinicians induce these changes without use of power techniques. Milton Erickson noted that every meeting with a client involves hypnotic induction. Indeed, on a subtle level clinicians powerfully affect clients in more ways than we might be consciously aware.

Somatic Therapies

Somatic therapies are the latest addition to trauma therapies. They have not been classified as power techniques, but they do have some common features. Somatic approaches are predicated upon the notion that therapeutic solutions reside in nonverbal methods of intervention. The zeal for these approaches may be well ahead of the data. Some of these therapies have connections to Gestalt, Rolfian, bioenergetic, and other approaches popular during the Esalen era. Present-day somatic therapies have appeal to biologically oriented clinicians. They reinforce the quest to "reset the amygdala," something that likely occurs spontaneously with other methods. Indeed, some of the single case examples and testimonials suggest there is potential in this approach. However, as with any new approach there are unknowns. Specifically, the somatic therapies run the risk of violating physical boundaries. Because of the physical touching, these approaches are more likely to harm complex trauma clients. I urge caution.

By the same token, I do not deny that "body memories" are real, and assisting clients in returning to a pre-traumatic biosensory balance is valuable. What is not clear is how much emphasis to place on this dimension. Clearly, a focus on grounding and dwelling in the emotional and physical present is of great clinical value. Somatic factors, either by design or default, are a necessary consideration in the quest for healing. I do advocate a very conservative approach, especially with addicted trauma clients.

Somatic Experiencing

Peter Levine, Ph.D., developed the somatic experiencing technique on the basis of prey animal observation. He noted that although regularly hunted, these animals recover quickly from life-threatening encounters. Levine speculated that animals have an innate mechanism to discharge the high levels of arousal generated by a near-death experience. He believed that these automatic mechanisms are overridden or inhibited by the rational levels of the human brain.

The remnant energy remains "stuck" in the nervous system, causing the disequilibrium observed in PTSD.

The somatic experience technique uses the body's awareness of sensation to help clients "renegotiate and heal their traumas rather than relive them." With this technique, Levine suggests that the "felt sense" permits the client to access a built-in immunity to traumatic reactions, permitting the hypothesized excess energy to be rebalanced, returning to a healthy equilibrium. Levine sees PTSD as an unresolved, overcharged response to threat frozen in time. His technique, somatic experiencing, claims to facilitate the "unthawing," resulting in a return to health, a heightened sense of reawakening, and reconnecting with the world.

Ensconced in rational but unproven neuroanatomical hypotheses, this method has some intrinsic appeal. Like the general foundations upon which trauma theory resides, this technique aspires to restore clients to a pre-traumatic, natural homeostasis. There appear to be Gestalt-like influences and even some Jungian undercurrents to this process. Levine's Web site states, for example, "People can open portals to rebirth and achieve an increased sense of aliveness and flow." The training and certification process is lengthy, requiring a three-year commitment.

Although enveloped in a nice-sounding theory, it is not clear that somatic experiencing has any particular advantage over more conventional methods, including relaxation training, cognitive-behavioral therapy, or some of the power techniques. In my opinion, the most powerful factor in this package is likely to be the emphasis upon safe, here-and-now sensations. As with hypnosis or relaxation training, the key variable is enhanced concentration on a particular focal point, oftentimes somatosensory. Whether this is a breakthrough technique or creative packaging is yet to be discerned. As with any technique, in the hands of a skilled clinician, outcomes are likely to be favorable. It will take extensive empirical investigation to sort out substantive, salient variable(s) for this technique.

Sensory Motor Psychotherapy

Sensory motor psychotherapy (SMP), developed by Pat Ogden, has become popular in recent years. Differing from somatic experiencing in its attempt to integrate multiple dimensions, SMP has some very good, complex core components. SMP advocates bottom-up (limbic) and top-down (cognitive) processing emphasizing cognitive skill building as well as increased somatic awareness. SMP borrows from Linehan's mindfulness construct, a core component of many Eastern religious disciplines.

SMP talks about assimilated versus unassimilated sensorimotor reactions. As stated by Ogden and Kekuni Minton (2000), "Bottom-up processing left on its own does not resolve trauma, but if the client is directed to employ the cognitive function of tracking and articulating sensorimotor experience while voluntarily inhibiting awareness of emotions, content, and interpretive thinking, sensorimotor experience can be assimilated."

The discerning reader will note the quoted words are slightly different, but the concepts are very similar to that which is advocated by cognitive-behavioral methods, DBT, and my own approach to therapy. Yet to be discerned is whether the packaging, vocabulary, or techniques have any unique advantage over other perhaps more conservative approaches. Outcome data is not yet available, and my concern, as with all somatic interventions, is the potential for mismatch of the access method and the client's severity or readiness for this type of approach. No doubt, there are valuable concepts and methods. The question remains in terms of efficacy. As with most techniques, in the hands of a good clinician, with conservative pacing, there are good but perhaps not necessarily unique components in SMP.

Teleology

As noted in chapter 4, teleology is the core of Viktor Frankl's *Man's Search for Meaning.* A philosophical and religious term with Greek origins, teleology refers to the destination, or endpoint. Teleology is what Frankl emphasizes as the factor that determines who shall live and who shall perish. Survivors of other horrors, including Bataan and the Gulags, independently validated Frankl's observations from the Nazi concentration camps.

Although widely read, Frankl's core observation, the power of teleology, never really became a popular therapeutic intervention. Perhaps it was timing, or perhaps it is the intimidating vocabulary. The fact of the matter is that there is an elegant simplicity in teleology, and it is easily applied as a potent factor in the process of therapy. Teleology is not a power technique per se, but it is definitely a profound intervention that can be of enormous benefit for clients suffering from trauma-based disorders, particularly those with complex trauma disorders.

In terms of application, teleological interventions are quite simple. Clients are asked to envision what they would do with freedom from intrusive symptoms. What is their fantasy in terms of meaningful application of their painfully gained wisdom? In other words, what role, action, or vision would give them meaning? What can they envision as providing meaning for them?

There are some parallels with solution-based therapy, but the vision and implications run deeper. Clients are asked to envision a future, one that is connected with others, and has purpose, direction, and meaning. This task requires them to envision a cessation of what I refer to as the inner civil war. I ask clients to articulate this vision and in some instances write it out. Early in recovery clients may not be able to articulate or even envision a positive possibility. This is okay, but it is important for the clinician to keep at it. In addition, it is helpful for the clinician to state something like: "It may not be clear to you yet, but I am confident you will find purpose and meaning as you get better. In the meantime, I just ask you to try to envision the possibility."

I then give clients some examples of how teleology works. Specifically, I ask them, "What is the best thing to do if you lose control of your car and begin to skid? You know you are about to hit a tree, so what do you do? The natural instinct is to slam on the brakes or quickly turn the wheel. Either of these choices will likely result in hitting the tree. The method taught to emergency rescue drivers, police officers, and race car drivers is to look toward where you want the car to go. When you do this, you seem to gently steer the car and, almost automatically, the car moves away from the tree, toward the direction of your gaze. (Do *not* try this at home.) In this example, you gain control. That is not really the objective. The real lesson is that you tend to go where you are looking."

I also tell clients the story of Anna O., who was actually an incest survivor named Bertha Pappenheim, one of the early clients described in analytic history. Anna O. was intensely treated and studied by Josef Breuer. Breuer tried to understand the symbols, dreams, and fantasies fueling Anna's so-called hysteria, but Breuer suddenly abandoned Anna when his wife made it clear she was jealous of his fascination with the patient. After this rejection, Anna regressed, returned to being mute, and remained institutionalized for several years. Anna finally realized that she needed to do something meaningful with her pain. She left the asylum, completed her education, and began a system of shelters and halfway houses for women who were sexually abused. The mute, depressed hysteric became an articulate feminist and pacifist. Her determination to help others ultimately proved to be the most powerful part of her recovery.

Another example I share with clients is Abraham Lincoln's response to the loss of his favorite son, William. Both Abe and Mary Todd, his wife, had already endured significant losses, but the untimely death of William in 1862 devastated them both. The role for grieving women of this era was to wear black and isolate themselves for a long period of time. Abe, on the other hand, was fully immersed in the Civil War. He chose to redirect his pain. He made a decision to do everything he could to bring the Civil War to an end. Further, he found meaning writing letters to families of fallen soldiers. It is not known if his grief was a factor in some of the pardons set forth for prisoners and deserters, but I suspect it was. Mary Todd, however, could not find a meaningful vision and the death of William was the beginning of her increasing depression, culminating in long periods of institutionalization. Even though there were likely other factors, having a purposeful vision seemed to have permitted Abe to function under unbelievable amounts of stress while his wife markedly deteriorated and never recovered.

It is not sufficient to use teleology with a client only once. Teleological intervention requires frequent repetition by the clinician. I tend to provide or prompt a teleological reminder once during each session, particularly with the most impaired clients. Another way to think about teleological intervention is to think of it as an antidote to the profound nihilism associated with severely impaired survivors. This is a much easier method of accessing the spiritual domain, without the profound resistance other approaches might engender. It provides the clinician a method of addressing hopelessness, perhaps the most daunting factor associated with treatment-resistant addicts and survivors.

Process

Recovery is a process that takes daily effort. Trauma-based disorders demand substantial effort to resolve. This effort does not always involve formal therapy. As with addictive disorders, some individuals get better over time by simply going to meetings, and some get better spontaneously. When therapy is involved, the process varies with every client. Duration and intensity of therapy are directly related to the severity of symptoms. Some clients respond well with very little intervention. More complex clients, who are more likely to have a concomitant addiction, tend to require a more substantial investment of time and effort. The process of therapy for this population requires that the clinician weave together a tapestry of techniques, supports, and additional resources, including Twelve Step work. No single technique or intervention will ensure success. As H. L. Mencken said, "For every complex problem, there is a solution that is simple, neat, and wrong." The following topics are factors to consider during the therapeutic process.

Interpretation

A simple lesson from graduate training: Even an inaccurate interpretation is better than no interpretation. I am not advocating reckless commentary. I am simply reminding the reader that absolute silence may increase anxiety.

As part of containment, compassion, and understanding, interpretive comments are usually soothing. I tend to favor simple, reassuring interpretations that remind the client that he or she was or felt helpless at the time of a trauma. I also tend to connect as many disparate processes and feelings as I can. I am not seeking absolute truth. Using an interpretive statement simply helps in terms of conceptual and verbal containment.

I definitely avoid classic Freudian interpretations or comments that would mystify or confuse. Whereas I might briefly refer to an unconscious process or comment on a theme such as, "That sounds like self-invalidating behavior. Why might you have engaged in it just then?" I almost always pose interpretation in the form of speculation or hypothesis building. I almost never make interpretive declarations such as, "So, this is what you felt and why you did that." Sensitive clients who have been verbally or sexually abused have had perpetrators define their reality. Clinicians must avoid any declarative interpretation that might sound controlling or declarative.

The Power of Summary

Summary is an opportunity to provide synthesis. I find that I summarize more often with clients who are more severely symptomatic. Summary provides reassurance, as well as a containment structure. Some clinicians tend to see summary as a mixed blessing. Many feel that a summary comment will interrupt the flow or impose our reality on the client. Yes, we do risk interrupting flow, but I have seen the general problem as providing too little commentary and summary.

Summarizing commentary is part of mirroring and demystifying. It is amazing how relieved a trauma client will feel by the clinician simply summarizing what was heard. Yes, this is part of active listening, but I believe we need to do it more often with trauma-based disorders. In addition, I strongly advocate multidimensional commentary and summary. Specifically, at the end of a session I will methodically comment on how the current events or old issues affected each dimension of the client's functioning. This is a simple, yet incredibly effective part of the therapy process.

Silence and Commentary

Silence is a classic therapy component that is powerful and necessary. A major aspect of our work involves active listening. In some traditional therapies and models, the balance of silence to commentary may not be appropriate for trauma-based clients. One of the more frequent complaints I hear from clients is, "My former therapist said nothing. He just listened and maybe said 'uh, huh.' That was about it."

I have found that trauma-related disorders almost demand a more active level of commentary, particularly during the early phases of therapy. Making observations, summarizing, and giving feedback, not direction, seems to soothe the fear and lessen the ambiguity. I found that silence potentiates anxiety and makes the client uncertain as to whether he or she is safe or being heard. In most instances I teach therapists, particularly those with traditional mental health backgrounds, to say more and say it sooner in the therapy process. Certainly, we spend the majority of our session listening, and I am not suggesting we lecture or chatter without focus. Too much silence feeds into a sense of mystery, which in some models helps build power and credibility. With trauma-based clients I see our major role as educator, not mystic. Yes, keep your power and indeed listen without comment, but recognize that the more you can synthesize, normalize, and say, the more likely you are to help build trust and provide much-needed clarity. Watch your tone. Be not parental, loud, insensitive, or sanctimonious. Speak with authority, but softly. Style matters.

Repetition, Repetition, Repetition

Congruent with my comments on summary, I find that clients with trauma-related disorders need more repetition than most. In general, the more impaired they are, the quicker they lose track of the larger picture. Whether you are aware of it or not, clinicians teach clients to see a larger, more synthesized and objective picture. We help with perspective as well as acceptance. More than most, trauma clients' "navigational" systems are thrown off by hypersensitivity, an overactive limbic system, and cognitive intrusion. I advocate summary and repetition of the overall goal as a means of redirecting. Repetition is part of a teleological intervention, the antidote to nihilistic negativity.

■

The process of therapy consists of more than just technique applied to symptoms. Clinical skill is an art form, not a collection of techniques. Learning technique is essential: We must learn the words and mechanics to the language of intervention. The process involves language and application, not just a simple declaration or incantation.

Clinical skills on a process level are difficult to teach. They must be honed over time, and the clinician must see differently, from multiple perspectives, integrate, and tolerate uncertainty. Involving much more than technique, it is more a function of beliefs, attitudes, inner grounding, and mastery of the basics. Process involves subtleties, style, timing, creativity, and integration. Strive to become a careful, conservative integrator of available techniques. Your style will evolve as long as you maintain good boundaries and healthy expectations.

Be careful not to feed into unnecessary mysticism or provide unrealistic promises. Our role is to guide, teach, contain, reframe, facilitate, but not control. Draw on all dimensions, listen with intensity, and speak with humility and wisdom. The twelve clinical principles in chapter 8 are complementary to an integrated therapeutic process.

■ ■ ■

CHAPTER SEVEN

ADDICTION AND TWELVE STEP INTEGRATION WITH TRAUMA DISORDERS

The multidimensional makeup of the Twelve Step model fits very well with the needs of survivors. Clients with both addictive disorders and trauma-related disorders often get better by just working the Twelve Steps. Many addicts recover from either or both disorders without formal treatment. This speaks to the brilliance, range, and depth of the Twelve Step program. The book *Glory Denied,* mentioned in chapter 4, describes the powerful story of Jim Thompson, a survivor of childhood abuse, alcoholism, and the longest and perhaps one of the most brutal stays in the Hanoi Hilton. A complex, heroic, and deeply injured man, Thompson was sober during the last ten years of his life with only the help of AA.

Many individuals with either or both conditions of addiction and PTSD require formal treatment. More severe cases of either illness will need more than peer support, meetings, and formal treatment. This is where professional training and thinking in both addiction and trauma can be lifesaving in terms of strategy, expectation, approach, resources, and language. When trauma-related disorders are involved, some powerful factors should be considered. Those factors concern timing, flexibility and acceptance, watching our choice of words, and using the Twelve Steps.

Timing

Timing is critical in different stages of treatment for PTSD and addiction. Some of the key timing issues are discussed in the following pages.

Get Sober First

Obvious to addiction professionals, mental health providers need to be disabused of the old illusion that if we treat the trauma, everything gets better. This is fantasy, not reality. Active using will invariably undo the best, most powerful, technically brilliant, insightful, and cathartic interventions. The old adage is true: What clients say when using has no therapeutic value. If it did, Veteran of Foreign War (VFW) posts would have become the main source of healing following our major wars.

Get the client into recovery. If we are dealing with a true addict, do not attempt treatment models designed for substance abusers. Few non-addicts are harmed if they go to meetings as the result of a misdiagnosis, but many addicts have died trying to fit the inaccurate diagnosis of substance abuser. Get your client sober, into treatment if needed, and stick with the gold standard of addiction recovery—a Twelve Step facilitation model.

Six-Month Window

Some addiction treatment providers adhere to a tradition of working exclusively on staying sober for the first year. The basic premise is this: "Work only the Steps, keep it simple, nothing complex, don't drink, and go to meetings." This tradition can be seriously misguided for clients with trauma-based disorders. Taken literally, some clients will use this advice as an excuse not to work on trauma-related issues. They focus only on substances, Step work, and meetings, using the well-intended declaration of addiction focus as an excuse to avoid dealing with trauma. Keep in mind that denial systems are operating for trauma-related disorders, not just addiction.

Clients need encouragement, sometimes prompting, and occasionally clear directives to work on underlying trauma during early recovery. We are not dealing with an either/or situation. Clients must work on both conditions formally or informally during the six-month window of opportunity. Clients in early recovery will likely relapse if they are not working on their trauma-related issues during the first six months of sobriety. Do not commit the clinical error of one-dimensional processing. Use the Steps, and add in the trauma disorder expertise (inpatient or outpatient) to facilitate simultaneous, intensive work on both conditions.

Which Step, When?

Introduce the Twelfth Step early, perhaps as early as during the First Step. Survivors can "think themselves stupid" just like any addict, and thinking ahead, not focusing on the here and now, is a hazard. The tradition of staying in the present is generally good, but clients with trauma-related disorders often need to think about the Twelfth Step even while they are doing their First Step. This is not blasphemy, but simple recognition of the fact that a focus upon a meaningful future can keep some clients, especially those with more severe trauma conditions, sober and motivated.

Keep in mind that clients whose trauma has affected spiritual systems and who suffer from a loss of meaning and hope need to see a possibility of having a purposeful recovery, one with meaning. Suggesting a vision of recovery and teaching the client about hope, giving back, and making a difference can be lifesaving.

Clearly, we don't want individuals in early recovery to act as junior counselors or actively apply the Twelfth Step. However, letting them know where they need to aim is a potent teleological intervention. The clinician needs to keep expectations realistic, but by the same token, it is inspiring to see a client's eyes come alive when he or she hears that others before them, perhaps even the clinician, have found meaning helping others recover from trauma and/or addiction. Giving back, in a moderate, temperate fashion, provides much-needed, and sometimes lifesaving, direction for clients who have embraced hopelessness and nihilism.

Clinician Flexibility and Acceptance

More than with most other client populations, clinicians working with addicted survivors need to be incredibly accepting and flexible. The firmness that some less complex addicts require can actually backfire with trauma-disorder clients.

Accept Relapse

We all know that relapse is part of the disease. However, the tough-love tradition has sometimes resulted in a rather black-and-white practice in some treatment centers or halfway houses. "If you use, you are out," some centers state. I am not suggesting that we become enablers and not act when a client relapses. However, what we do or fail to do can have profound consequences. Clients with trauma-based disorders may not be using as a function of defiance or using for the sake of using. In some instances the relapse is a function of triggering. So, be careful about your assumptions concerning relapse. Many relapses have trauma underpinnings. No, that does not provide an excuse for using, but we need to be careful not to engage in contempt prior to investigation, judgmentalism, or black-and-white thinking.

If your program is not designed to treat dual disorders, do not simply kick the client out; instead send him or her to another level of care, one that can deal with trauma issues. At my facility, we take relapse very seriously, do not minimize it, and have some clearly delineated consequences regarding relapse. We do not automatically discharge a client simply because he or she has relapsed. However, relapse in most instances is seen as an opportunity for new work, healthful confrontation about the addiction, humility, and new understanding about possible trauma connections to the relapse. Keep in mind, we are dealing with two cognitive paradigms: the urge to use and victim-based thinking.

Tolerate Manipulation

Making addicts aware of their deceptiveness, self-deceptiveness, and manipulation is vital. Some clients can handle direct feedback and thrive on the clarity. However, clients with trauma disorders, and especially those with more severe symptoms, do not consciously recognize many of these behaviors. Directly confronting some of these issues can do more harm than good. I have found that I need more patience for more injured clients. Clients with more injury are more vulnerable to a confrontation. Yes, they need the feedback, but style and timing must be considered when we have wounded clients. The clinician must be diplomatic, accepting, gentle, and tolerant. The clinician must get clients to recognize their manipulations, sometimes having to wait patiently for clients to derive their own answers. In the long run, gentle interpretation and mild questioning tend to be more effective than confrontation.

Manipulation must be identified by the clinician, but do not let frustration provoke you to confront harshly when patience is needed. How do you know when to be tolerant and when to confront directly? There is no absolute formula, but in general, the greater the client injury, the more the need for clinician frustration tolerance. It is okay to get manipulated. As some colleagues have stated, “The client is being a client.”

Word Choice

Language is incredibly powerful. The words we choose can set tone, expectation, resistance, or compliance. Not all listeners hear the same thing, and the words that may be benign for some have deleterious consequences for others. Addicts with survivor issues often have powerful reactions to words that many addiction counselors take for granted, see as benign, or view as positives. When working with survivor clients, it is important to consider how certain words might affect these individuals.

"Powerless"

This potent word permits addicts to let go of the illusion of control over their addiction. However, to a survivor, the word may have a different meaning. Being powerless is what individuals with trauma-based disorders fear and despise most. They may on some level recognize they are indeed powerless over events, but they have not yet come to terms with their inability to control the outcome of trauma-related circumstances.

In PTSD parlance, we must remember the concept of "magical thinking." This refers to the almost psychotic level of distortion involving control over specific events. The classic example is the client who says to himself or herself: "I should have called 911." In a current circumstance, calling 911 might make sense, but many clients will make this comment in reference to events that occurred decades before the 911 system was in place. Rationality is sacrificed in terms of memory.

This distortion fits the internal perception that the client never should have lost control. "Don't confuse me with the facts" is an attitude the clinician may encounter. The need to hold on to the illusion of control is extremely powerful with clients who have not yet accepted themselves, their lack of control, and the reality that control is an illusion. Therefore, counselors must be careful when the word "powerless" is applied.

In general, we can instruct the client that this word pertains only to the chemical(s) of choice and addiction. However, we need to quickly interpret that we will be moving toward a wider integration of the concept of powerlessness. Simply interpreting and respecting the fact that there are additional implications to the word often lowers clients' anxiety over this potent, core word.

"Surrender"

The word "surrender" also tends to have a different meaning to clients with trauma-based disorders. Again, simply recognizing that the term may have larger meaning helps to reduce fear. It should be obvious that the request to surrender would cause considerable fear, resistance, and perhaps anger from a client with PTSD.

"Acceptance"

Acceptance is a tremendously daunting challenge and speaks to the core of recovery from both conditions. It is helpful to limit and define acceptance around the addiction first. The counselor can inform the client that the range of acceptance will expand as the client works the Twelve Steps, gets stronger, and works through the trauma-based issues.

I often tell clients, "Acceptance is a big issue, and I don't expect us to be able to deal with it all at once. Think of acceptance first in terms of addiction; however, as we move forward we will look at acceptance in terms of the painful events of your past. Just to let you know, self-acceptance is the core issue for most survivors. Most individuals have a hard time accepting the limits of their control and the need to embrace forgiveness of self."

"Forgiveness"

The main difficulty with the word "forgiveness" is the expectation that the perpetrators must be forgiven. Although this is a Judeo-Christian-based tradition, it does not work well with most survivors. We need to lower the level of expectation on this, since many survivors cannot forgive their perpetrators. It helps to inform clients that they can get better without forgiving the perpetrator or only partially forgiving him or her. Absolute forgiveness may be unrealistic and even inappropriate. However, self-forgiveness is essential. Most survivor symptoms are fueled by a lack of self-forgiveness.

"Personality Defect"

Trauma-based clients do not usually have a hard time with the words "character defects" or "shortcomings." Talking about character or personality defects, as opposed to the Axis II nomenclature (personality disorders), usually makes it easier to focus on blind spots in terms of perception and behavior. Since all people and all addicts have personality defects, this choice of words is most often acceptable. However, some of the most sensitive trauma-based clients resent the term. A part of their internal reality sees themselves as all perfect and completely defective. Thus, engaging in any endeavor to explore their role in events current or past can be threatening. The clinician may simply choose to say: "This is an issue involving the Fourth Step, and we are not yet ready to go there. However, survivors who transcend are able to admit imperfection. This is not self-condemning but involves the process of self-acceptance and coming to terms with what is realistic, not ideal."

The Twelve Steps

Specific Steps can raise powerful issues with some trauma clients. In this section we will look at issues that might arise when these clients work specific Steps and what the clinician needs to do in order to manage the resistance.

Step One: We admitted we were powerless over alcohol—that our lives had become unmanageable.

Clients with trauma-based disorders can misinterpret the word "powerless." The clinician needs to emphasize that we are focusing only on addiction, and this is not a general declaration of powerlessness, even though in some ways it really is. Step One can be threatening in many respects. It suggests that clients are not unique, do not have complete control, and are committing to a process that may take away what they perceive as their only tool for dealing with profound pain. The clinician may wish to consider some of the following suggestions:

- Acknowledge: Acknowledge that the First Step's focus on powerlessness can get confused with victimization issues from the past.
- Disarm the fear: Remind clients that fear and resentment are part of the internal addict, who is looking to manipulate them into remaining a de facto victim and a victim of addiction's many illusions.
- Empower: Reinforce the client's desire to remain strong, but remind him or her that even the strongest have certain limits.
- Inform: Remind clients that no addict can use simple willpower to control his or her disease.
- Validate: Validate the complexity of clients' backgrounds. Remind them that they are unusual or different in some ways but are ordinary when it comes to the disease of addiction.
- Separate the problems: Trauma-disorder addicts have two issues to face: addiction and the trauma disorder. Clients must first focus on the addiction, and as they progress through the Steps, the separate yet often connected issues of trauma can be discussed. You may wish to designate someone to specialize in each problem, even though sometimes there is overlap. However, the designated expert, counselor, sponsor, or therapist is the primary guide for his or her specialty issue.

- Simplify and demystify: The counselor or therapist might say something like: "Keep it simple and let's continue to work on the process where you reclaim reality and not dwell in a world of imagined control."
- Anchor in the present and empower: Reinforce that the ultimate goal of this process is to make clients stronger, and the real agenda is to assist them in reclaiming a here-and-now reality.

Step Two: Came to believe that a Power greater than ourselves could restore us to sanity.

Most clinicians are familiar with how to deal with resistance to a Higher Power. Addicts with trauma disorders may have fear- and anger-based issues, and some may be more prone toward agnosticism or atheism.

- Reflect and identify the resistance: The clinician may need to reflect to clients that giving power to another may not fit their intuition. Anyone or any concept having power can be frightening for survivors.
- Redirect: Remind addict survivors that the chemicals generate insanity as well. What they feel is not just the residual of abuse or abandonment by their Higher Power, but the chemical has done injury to them.
- Normalize: It is helpful to state directly that many survivors feel betrayed, and if clients are feeling this, it is normal.
- Clarify: Remind clients that they do not have to "submit," pledge faith, or become religious.
- Future expectation: The concept of surrender will feel less frightening as time in recovery increases. Remind clients that their emotional pain will diminish going forward.
- Language: Remind clients that the goal is not resolution, but essentially an internal ceasefire. Once the internal ceasefire is in effect, you will help them sort out the confusing inner language, and this will eventually help them find peace with their Higher Power issues.
- Insight: Remind clients that the goal of recovery and therapy is to help them sort out their distortions. It is the distortion process that continues to keep the abuse and chaos alive. Separating the symptom from themselves is highly empowering.

- Confront the extreme: Remind clients that we are not looking for absolute answers. The goal is to disentangle reality from illusion, and their nihilism may be one of those illusions.

***Step Three: Made a decision to turn our will and our lives over to the care of God* as we understood Him.**

It is helpful for the clinician to point out arcane or sexist language. Whereas the enlightened clinician may assume no comment is necessary, sexual abuse survivors in particular tend to have difficulty with language that is sexist, even in a historical context, such as the use of the pronoun "Him" in Step Three.

- Empower: Remind clients that those who have made this journey before have gained power, not control. Remind clients that you have faith in them and the process.
- Interpret: Turning one's will over to God does not mean passivity. It does mean that with this Step clients will strive to hear God's message as spoken to them through others. This helps to balance the need to let go and reinforces the survivor's need to hear feedback from peers, therapist, and sponsor.

Step Four: Made a searching and fearless moral inventory of ourselves.

This can be a particularly daunting Step for individuals with trauma-based disorders. Since clients tend to believe that they caused all that went wrong, committing to paper a moral inventory is truly a challenge. Be careful that clients do not immerse themselves in a toxic episode of self-blame or self-abuse. It is very important to remind clients not to interpret the task in a black-and-white fashion. Let them know that admitting flaws is difficult, especially for survivors of abuse. Since boundaries get so readily confused, remind clients that the purpose of this Step is to help better define themselves separately from the events, not dwell on their own perceived shortcomings.

Encourage clients to be as nonjudgmental as possible. Acceptance of the goal and moving forward with self-forgiveness is really the intended outcome. Acknowledge that they may have played a role in what went wrong, but continue to remind clients that they are not that powerful. Accepting one's role is healthy, but guilt immersion is not productive. Other suggestions include the following:

- Language: Encourage clients to not take the word "moral" at face value. It may be helpful to translate the word to mean being thorough and honest.
- Expectation: One of the structures for the Fourth Step used in the Big Book asks the addict to take an inventory of (1) fears, (2) resentments, and (3) sexuality in relation to others. It may be helpful to create the expectation that the task of categorizing and listing may prevent emotional flooding. Writing is a great method of gaining distance from emotion, and completing this Step is likely to make clients less vulnerable to the tyranny of intense emotion and guilt.
- Normalize: Remind clients that this is a difficult Step for almost everyone. Repeat the first definition of PTSD (found on page 18) that normalizes and reminds clients that many survivors hurt others before they get better. It is not that all victims become perpetrators, but sometimes the pain gets transformed, injuring innocent parties and loved ones.
- Future focus: Inform clients that the intent of Step Four is not to immerse oneself in self-loathing, but it is preparation for forgiveness and acceptance. Subsequent Steps will move in this direction.
- Containment: It is very important to create an expectation that completing this Step does not require reliving the past or retrieving every memory. It is helpful to remind clients that some individuals repeat this Step. It is not always realistic to get it all the first time through.

Step Five: Admitted to God, to ourselves, and to another human being the exact nature of our wrongs.

Many of the caveats for Step Four are applicable here as well. In addition, I would suggest that the clinician remind clients that magical thinking (taking blame for everything) is part of PTSD and is not what this Step is about. It may also be helpful to reframe self-blame as an addictive behavior.

Remind clients that they are not expected to be perfect. Tolerating imperfection is different from engaging in self-blame. Remind them that self-blame is a reflex for younger survivors and that many perpetrators manipulate victims by reinforcing blame. Reassure clients that you and others are their advocates. Finally, remind clients to remember the positives and recite their positive self-statements, and not just obsess about what went wrong.

Step Six: Were entirely ready to have God remove all these defects of character.

Step Seven: Humbly asked Him to remove our shortcomings.
Both Steps Six and Seven are God Steps. Survivor addicts need to be reminded that despite their history, instinct, and victim thinking, they are not the source of all that went wrong. Nor are they the source of all healing. These Steps focus on letting go and do not require personal action. These Steps can be daunting for agnostic or atheistic survivors. Passivity is an anathema, and letting go is a huge challenge.

Remind clients that they do not need to become believers in order to work these Steps. They only need to believe that things can get better, that there is hope, and that they will definitely find their own personal meaning, focus, and purpose as they let go of old behaviors and attitudes. Since God is a personal experience, it is not the words but the attitude that matters. Letting go requires a shift in attitude as well as recognizing they are not always in control. Self-acceptance and self-forgiveness can be incorporated. Some trauma clients benefit from meetings with other agnostics, and this may need to be introduced as an acceptable alternative.

Step Eight: Made a list of all persons we had harmed, and became willing to make amends to them all.

Step Nine: Made direct amends to such people wherever possible, except when to do so would injure them or others.
These can be difficult Steps for many survivors. Addicts with PTSD tend to interpret these Steps as a demand to forgive the perpetrators. Indeed, they are not. Despite the Judeo-Christian belief that we must always honor parents, and the Christian tradition of forgiving or praying for those who have injured you, these Steps are not making such a blanket demand.

Steps Eight and Nine involve making amends to those we have harmed during addiction and can be so-limited. Even if there is ambiguity, as there often is, about who is a perpetrator and who is a victim, these Steps should not feed into the distortion that blanket apologies and amends are made to those who have harmed the client. The clinician may wish to carefully focus these two Steps upon damage done to others by the addiction only.

I tend to focus Steps Eight and Nine on making amends to *self* as well as others, "except when to do so would injure . . . others." For example, for someone who has been sexually promiscuous while in a committed relationship, confessing and apologizing to one's partner may bring harm to that partner. In this case, the client needs to work out the issues of guilt confidentially before considering "apologizing."

It is also wise for the clinician to exempt certain individuals, like the perpetrators, from the list of those to whom the client needs to make amends. This is a clinician's judgment call and should be tailored to the client's needs and readiness. The tradition for Step Nine provides a wise exemption or "loophole," that is, "except when to do so would injure them or others." For clients with trauma-based disorders, their amends list should include themselves.

Step Ten: Continued to take personal inventory and when we were wrong promptly admitted it.

Most clients who have reached this Step have disabused themselves of the self-blame game, but a reminder might be advisable. Continue to encourage the process of self-forgiveness and point out when or if the self-loathing reemerges. Reminders to continue the repetition of positive self-statements may be of value, along with a daily inventory before bed, so that the inventory is made and finished, one day at a time.

Step Eleven: Sought through prayer and meditation to improve our conscious contact with God* as we understood Him, *praying only for knowledge of His will for us and the power to carry that out.

If a survivor has traveled this far, Step Eleven does not tend to create obstacles. Again, the fairness aspect and the concept of God may need to be rearticulated in terms of perceived abandonment by one's Higher Power. It is good to remind clients that prayer does not mean good outcome or control.

I tend to say things like: "We seek insight, clarity, and acceptance, not perfect control or omniscience. Safety is still a big item and prayer does not guarantee this, nor is it a substitute for instinct. Vigilance is okay, but hypervigilance is a waste of consciousness and biological energy. I encourage you to become more meditative and self-reflective as your foundations continue to strengthen. Conscious contact is another means of empowerment, not control. Recovery from traumatic events requires top-down and bottom-up strategies. Cognition is one piece, but conscious contact taps into that next level up, however we understand it. There is evidence to support a neurobiological basis for spirituality and the benefits of meditation or prayer. This is part of our wiring and Step Eleven facilitates this dimension of the integration process."

You may wish to show the client figure 7, the four-dimensional grid from page 68 in chapter 4. Seeing this image can be helpful.

Step Twelve: Having had a spiritual awakening as the result of these steps, we tried to carry this message to alcoholics, and to practice these principles in all our affairs.

Embracing a realistic vision of the Twelfth Step early in recovery can be an invaluable source of hope for trauma-disorder clients. The teleological vision, or finding meaning from the chaos, can be a profoundly powerful recovery factor. Some survivors strive for perfection and believe that they must become helping professionals. Clearly, this is not mandated, although many do make this choice.

Realistic expectations, not grandiose or fantasy-based demands, are what the Twelfth Step really asks for. I also remind survivors that they cannot control others. Some die from the disease of addiction, and not all trauma survivors want to or can be helped.

In addition, I remind them that boundaries are vital. Whether they become sponsors, speakers, researchers, or clinicians, they as survivors must continue to pay attention to triggers and their possible negative effect on objective judgment and/or boundaries. I might suggest the following caveat: "Never, never act beyond the scope of the program. You might be tempted, but ask others before you do anything that might be seen by others as heroic. Helping is not rescuing, and working the Twelfth Step should not become an excuse to flirt with chaos again. That temptation is always there, so be patient, and stick with your training and tradition. Do not even contemplate bending or breaking the rules. We need helpers, not martyrs."

■

Twelve Step integration and trauma recovery follow parallel paths. Clinicians need to be sensitive to different perceptions held by addicts struggling with trauma-related disorders. Some of the language and assumptions applied to less complex addicts need reconsideration and balanced articulation. Be sensitive to the possibility that more complex clients will get stuck on some Steps and some key words. Rather than losing patience, the clinician must develop greater patience and clarity. Watch the language and be careful of individual client's misinterpretations of certain slogans or standard recovery expectations. If your client gets stuck, consider how the themes of abuse, neglect, betrayal, and violence may be distorting his or her interpretation of specific words or Steps.

The words I used as examples of how to speak with clients now flow with ease, but they took me many years to develop. The exact words aren't as important as your recognition that survivors, especially complex survivors, may not see or hear things the same way as other addicts. We are our clients' guides in this process of integration, with and around the Twelve Steps.

■ ■ ■

CHAPTER EIGHT

TWELVE CLINICAL PRINCIPLES

Treating addicts with trauma-based disorders requires knowledge of and specific sensitivity to post-traumatic dynamics and issues. Standard approaches are often inadequate and fail to address the complexity and contradiction associated with these compelling clients. Clinicians can enhance their efficacy by adhering to some fairly simple guidelines. In my opinion, attitude, perspective, flexibility, and conceptual framework can be more powerful than specific techniques. The clinician must strive to be accepting, nonjudgmental, directive, soothing, rational, hopeful, and infinitely patient.

A super clinician is not necessarily needed to help these clients; however, the wider your knowledge about what to do or what not to do and the greater your flexibility, the less likely you are to feed into the internal agenda oriented toward client self-blame. Be careful of jargon from both the addiction and recovery worlds. Labels and addiction slogans can do harm to some of the more complex clients. Keep in mind that we are dealing with bilingual individuals: The addict speaks a language that is often different from that of the victim.

Successful work with survivor clients who also have an addiction requires many considerations. I have selected twelve core principles that will assist clinicians working with complex clients. Much of what I am suggesting draws on classic approaches, but some of the material that follows is of my own derivation and synthesis.

Clinical Principle 1: Validation

Validating a survivor is an art form. It is not as simple as saying, "I understand." In fact, many generic statements of comfort can be seen as insincere, superficial, and invalidating. Soothing and reassuring someone going through acute grief is difficult. Most people do not know what to do or say. Avoid clichés, platitudes, and being trite. Even the generic "aha" or "uh-huh" responses can be seen as superficial, inattentive, and ineffective.

I tend to validate and soothe clients with a brief introduction that goes something like this: "I am pleased you are here. Most people I see are struggling with relapse, recovery, and trauma. I think I know a little about trauma issues, but I certainly don't know what has hurt you. I am going to listen as best I can to what you are struggling with. Just to let you know, I can't fix it, since there is no cure for this kind of pain. However, I can help you understand it, better manage it, and coexist with it. Has anyone told you what exactly post-traumatic stress disorder is? If not, then let me explain."

I then recite one or more of the PTSD definitions based upon timing, instinct, and circumstance. I go on to explain that my role is to help declare an end to an internal civil war. I am careful to state that the client has ultimate choice and I am there as a facilitator/advocate. I'll say, "This process takes tenacity and clarity, and I intend to stay with it for as long as you permit. My work with many survivors before has shown me there is sometimes an agenda where you may want me to join in the hopelessness. That is not my mission. I have seen others get better and that is my hope for this process. Ultimately, it is your choice, but I will do my best to tell you the truth as I see it."

Not sounding trite can be challenging. Sometimes silence is most appropriate, and if in doubt, simply listen. Point out to the client that self-forgiveness is a long-term goal. When a traumatic event is recalled, remind the client that self-blame is the typical internal default. I might outright declare, "It wasn't your fault," knowing and stating full well that this will not be readily believed. It is necessary for the clinician to intermittently repeat: "It is not possible to control unmanageable events."

On occasion, it is helpful to use humor or irony as a tool of soothing or validating. I might sardonically say, "Well, we all know you are responsible for this." Obviously, this technique should be employed with great conservatism and only after a full therapeutic trust level has been established. In general, the clinician can best soothe the survivor by active listening and then reminding him or her that it is possible to find meaning going forward.

Clinical Principle 2: Confront Victim Thinking

Effective clinical work with survivors requires more than just empathy. It is important for the clinician to point out gently, but sometimes assertively, when the client is regressing toward victim thinking. Simply point out that he or she may have been triggered. More specifically, I try to keep the situation on an objective footing by using language such as, "It appears that maybe you were triggered, and your limbic system has taken over. As we have discussed before, the residual fear can override objectivity and logic. Let's try to look at what really happened yesterday and see how it might be connected to traumatic underpinnings. The more we can take away the mystery, the less often your consciousness will be hijacked by shadows of the past or, more simply, your limbic system."

I also try to remind the client that dissociation (numbness) and anger are most often the default conditions. When triggered, the most common consequence is an outburst of anger and profound feelings of mistrust. Sudden surges of anger are very often an indication of triggering and regression to limbic thinking and the substrate for full-blown victim thinking.

When clients have been triggered and cannot be soothed or do not respond rationally to the suggestion that victim thinking is occurring, it is helpful to point out the dramatic shift in emotional state and then remind them that this is not typical or desirable. If the situation is not interrupted, it will "fulfill the need for self-invalidation. You will continue to be angry and push away your sponsor, spouse, roommate, or whomever. This has been part of your pattern, and it feeds right into feeling alone, unworthy, and unique. We talked about this before, and it is a version of 'terminal uniqueness.' Chaos loves this, and you have a history of being a chaos junkie. Now, I am not saying that I know with certainty that your perceptions are off, but are others also seeing what you are? If you are the only one this upset, angry, and offended, it may be helpful to consider whether this is classic victim thinking. You really need to resist the seduction of chaos. Being a survivor is much more manageable than continuing to be a victim."

Generally speaking, the clinical objective is to reempower cognition and choice. Being frightened, angry, righteously indignant, and terminally unique are not very empowering or powerful positions. Looking at the connection between state, trigger, perception, and circumstance is what therapy is all about.

Clinical Principle 3: Simultaneity of Twelve Step Participation and Trauma Treatment

Despite some potential linguistic differences, it is absolutely essential that clients with both disorders participate in recovery meetings. Sometimes seen as an afterthought by individual clinicians and some treatment programs, ongoing AA or NA involvement is vital in terms of sobriety and is helpful in terms of trauma recovery. Transcending the aspects of uniqueness and the instinct toward isolation is part of what Step work requires. Confronting powerlessness and acceptance are difficult hurdles and can become a part of the process of trauma transcendence. In addition, simply going to meetings forces clients to deal with other people and begin building a support system.

It is vital to have both Step work and trauma work happening at the same time. Discontinuation of Step work is a setup for a relapse in most instances, and this vital work should not be de-emphasized. A good clinician will welcome both Twelve Step and trauma treatment. The reality is that victim or addiction thinking can undermine recovery and result in relapse. Cognitive distortions or victim-entitlement thinking can have identical behavioral consequences. To make it even trickier, these distortions can be almost automatic, that is, functioning outside the awareness of the client. The sharp clinician can anticipate these distortions on either a conscious or unconscious level. If the clinician is thinking only in one language, the probability of detecting these distortions is greatly diminished.

Another way to think of trauma work is that, properly implemented, it is a vital part of relapse prevention. In fact, I suspect that the vast majority of people who chronically relapse have not received the needed treatment for trauma-related disorders. Relapse prevention paradigms cover some of this domain but not with sufficient clarity or specificity. The cognitive-behavioral mechanics of relapse prevention are vital but will not work unless trauma-related themes are identified and defused as an identified clinical goal. As noted previously, the cognitions of victim thinking are difficult to detect unless you are listening and processing the client's cognitions/behaviors in those terms. Cognitive distortions that facilitate relapse can be either addiction thinking or victim thinking, and in some instances, both. I sometimes refer to this as "the unholy tag team." Therefore, the cognitive-behavioral constructs of relapse prevention can be dramatically enhanced if the clinician is thinking in terms of the language of the victim. Although it sounds simple, simultaneous therapy is not often done. I am a strong advocate of simultaneous Step work and trauma therapy.

A final thought on integration: When a client tells the clinician about a particularly troubling event, encourage him or her to share it with his or her sponsor and peers, when the time is right. The disclosure has more power once it is shared with others. Whether we see this as habituation, abreaction, group process, or desensitization, it helps enormously when others have been informed. Part of the magic of recovery is disabusing one's self of the secrecy. AA and NA's emphasis upon disclosure and telling one's story helps take away the mystery and power of trauma-related themes. In addition, clients attending meetings will hear others talk about their traumas (since about one-third of attendees are also survivors). This fits nicely in terms of universality, acceptance, and letting go of uniqueness. For survivors, there is nothing quite as empowering as hearing another person talk about similar issues, events, and emotions. The sigh of relief is almost audible.

Clinical Principle 4: Self-Affirmation and Self-Acceptance

Clients with trauma-related disorders need to be reminded that one of the main goals of therapy is self-acceptance. I have mentioned the value of positive self-statements, but they are not a panacea. However, since many clients engage in daily self-loathing, encouraging and reminding them to repeat positive statements can be very helpful.

More important, the process of self-acceptance involves aspects of acceptance embedded in the Steps. We are dealing with a goal of transcendent self-acceptance. In fact, several years ago I had a flash (not as profound as Bill W.'s) and saw the following phrase while I was working with a client: *"Transcendent self-acceptance is the key to treating repetitive and compulsive self-invalidation."* I have actually asked clients to write down this statement and repeat it on occasion. They report that my recitation of this phrase or their rereading it is helpful. It is easy to lose sight of the larger goal, especially when triggering occurs.

Clinical Principle 5: The Cognitive-Behavioral Mantra: Contain, Reframe, Refocus

Easy to remember and easy to teach, this "mantra" can be very useful to clinician and client. Part of our mission is to teach coping skills. Recitation of this simple refrain can assist a client who has been triggered.

Clients still stuck in the victim mode do not live with this mantra. The victim mantra is more like: flood, dissociate, spread negativity. The core problem is that victims do not have good boundary skills. As clinicians, we need to be role models and teach useful skills. When the client has encountered a trigger, a simple reminder of the cognitive-behavioral mantra can be soothing and salutary. I usually introduce the mantra before a crisis has erupted, and this way I can refer back to it when an episode has occurred. In some instances I ask clients to write out the mantra and carry it with them as an anchoring tool when they feel a sudden emotional shift.

Contain

As mentioned in chapter 4, clients in early recovery should be taught *not* to trust their gut reactions. That is because when triggering occurs, raw fear shuts down cognition. Under more benign conditions, "trust your gut" encourages instinct to enhance thinking. For clients with trauma-based disorders, the intrusion of fear is so potent that it interrupts rational choice. The cognitive-behavioral mantra is a reminder that there are choices, not just gut reactions.

This clinical directive to "contain" is not the same as dissociate, although there are some common features. Dissociation is containment gone awry. Containment means you have awareness, have not gone totally flat, and are not in an altered state. Containment is not control either. It simply means that the ripples of emotional distortion (panic) are not determining thought and behavior. Containment represents the midpoint between emotional flooding and dissociation. It is the observer's perspective, one where you feel the emotions, see the event, but you are not overwhelmed. I teach clients to employ relaxation techniques, grounding, and other components of their "toolbox" to contain the emotionality. In some instances a power technique may be needed to solidify this process.

Reframe

Reframing is an ubiquitous clinical process all clinicians are familiar with. I find it more empowering to ask clients to derive the words or imagery of reframing rather than my imposing it. I might need to do it for them the first time, but subsequently, most clients become very good at reframing. Interestingly, they tend to forget to do this unless the clinician reminds them.

Refocus

Refocusing refers to more of a teleological (forward-looking) perspective. While *reframing* is more of a here-and-now reinterpretation of what has occurred, *refocusing* reminds the client to look ahead toward meaningfulness. The challenge of refocusing is to remind clients to visualize how they want to take the intensity that has just been triggered and use it toward a larger vision, one that involves a future. Remember that the sense of foreshortened future operates on fear. Reminding clients that there are possibilities of refocusing their intensity toward pro-social goals can make a huge contribution in shutting off the mechanisms of limbic fear. Simply stated, refocusing can be a simple recitation of the larger, long-term goal. This is not projecting ahead, as so many addicts engage in. It is simply recommitting to a vision of serenity, purpose, and meaning.

Recitation of the cognitive-behavioral mantra can be a shortcut and a reminder of some complex clinical themes as well as a restatement of a vision toward hope and recovery. It is a simple tool with considerable power.

Clinical Principle 6: Triggers: Anticipation, Normalization, and Preparation

For the client, I demystify the clinical process as one not of psychoanalysis but of, more important, "trigger analysis." By simplifying and demystifying the clinical process, the client is likely to be more comfortable. This process puts the client on a more equal footing with the therapist rather than reinforcing the clinician as the "mystical fixer."

By describing the main task as trigger identification or trigger analysis, the clinician is defining the therapeutic goal as an acquisition of applied skill. This is congruent with what Edna Foa, Francine Shapiro, and others refer to as "skill instillation." I strive to keep a balance of expectancy and egalitarianism. That is, I remain the authority, but I employ the client as an equal participant in the healing process.

I also make it clear that what we do in the therapy session has little relevance if the skills are not utilized in the real world between sessions. I ask clients to keep a triggering events journal. In this manner they become more aware of what events, transparent or symbolic, result in an "episode." I emphasize that the more conscious this process becomes, the more empowered they will become. Clearly, this does not result in "control" since that is an illusion.

I inform clients that it is not at all unusual that they will experience unconscious triggers, but I suggest that there is almost always an identifiable event. I also let clients know that being triggered is okay (normalization). Clients are not expected to anticipate all triggers, nor will they interpret things with accuracy without experience.

In terms of preparation, encourage clients to develop a personal "toolkit," which includes skills of breathing, relaxation, meditation, grounding, transitional objects, safe imagery, and so on. It is most empowering to teach these skills when clients are not triggered; then encourage them to use these skills in real-world settings. In some instances, practice is helpful, and this is perhaps why exposure techniques are becoming popular again. Most important, the client must become skilled in applying various techniques in real-world settings. I frequently ask my clients to have certain tools with them at all times, to be used if triggered. These can include transitional objects; positive self-statements (written by them); the survivor's serenity prayer (found below); a prepared message to one's "limbic self"; the picture of a safe person, protector, or pet; phone numbers of a sponsor and rational peers; a personal prayer; and the cognitive-behavioral mantra.

Serenity Prayer for Survivors

God, grant me the serenity to seek balance,
The courage to find meaning,
And the wisdom to forgive myself.

I composed the Serenity Prayer for Survivors in order to facilitate focus and awareness on an insight that tends to be readily forgotten. Some clients find it awkward upon first recitation, but with repeated use it speaks to the core of what addicts with survivor issues need to remember.

I also remind clients that on occasion, they may feel overwhelmed despite all the tools. Teach clients that it is okay if this happens and that the episode will subside. They must be encouraged not to make decisions when they feel anger, panic, or absolute flatness (dissociation). Going numb for a while is also okay. Temporary dissociation is all right as long as critical decisions are not made during this distorted but nonmystical state.

Finally, remind clients of the four-dimensional grid (figure 7 in chapter 4). Encourage clients to examine where they are in terms of the four dimensions (psychological, spiritual, biological, and interpersonal). For example, using the biological quadrant, if a client has not eaten or slept, work with him or her to determine what is helpful versus what is self-destructive.

Asking them to look at cognitive distortions, the instinct to isolate, and spiritual distortions is an incredibly powerful method of interrupting a triggering episode. Using multidimensional concepts and teaching this skill is highly empowering.

Clinical Principle 7: Teleological Intervention

Teleology, or setting one's vision toward a future goal, can be seen as a variant of spirituality. The main difference is that for teleology, a Higher Power concept need not be a formal part of the picture. This makes a teleological intervention less threatening for survivors who have not yet made peace with the God of their vision.

As mentioned previously, many survivors, who feel blessed and cursed all at once, have issues of abandonment or anger toward their Higher Power. Many simply tolerate the language and concepts, but secretly exempt themselves because God did not protect them or prevent a tragedy from occurring. An easy therapeutic starting point is to invoke the legacy and gift of Viktor Frankl, a Nazi concentration camp survivor. Even the most "terminally unique," injured, entitled, or recalcitrant survivor will listen to the voice of someone who survived the most horrific experience anyone can imagine.

To some extent, Frankl's background permits us to "outrank," if you will, the inner voice and dynamic of an active victim who might believe "nobody understands and nobody had it rougher than me." If the individual clinician even attempts to directly challenge this inner voice, invalidation is immediate. You cannot safely say to a client with a trauma-based disorder, "Stop feeling sorry for yourself and get over it." This statement will almost always backfire. It is safer to say, "You are being victimized by limbic thinking. You may be engaging in victim thinking. You may have been triggered. Let's examine this." Remember we must do no harm. Careful language is vital, and we must not invalidate the client, but by the same token, we must challenge pathology.

Using teleological strategies permits us to transcend many limitations. We can safely point to a survivor of incredible, unequivocal stature, use him or her as a role model, and then employ the spiritual dimension in a more benign fashion.

Now, with all of that, how do we employ teleology? First, teach the client what the word means. Next, I almost always ask my clients to read Frankl's book *Man's Search for Meaning,* perhaps one of the most profound books of the twentieth century. It is remarkably simple and powerful. After the client has read it, we then discuss its relevance to his or her own situation. Only the most recalcitrant client will fail to identify and feel some relief after reading Frankl. The problem is that the relief is transitory, and feelings of hopelessness quickly rekindle. This is why repetition of the definitions of trauma and addiction, the first steps for both, is so vital.

Insight and understanding are important but fleeting. How many times have you seen pictures of starving children and felt gratitude for the circumstances of your own life, only to get upset about a minor loss, like a dent in your new car? People forget life-changing insights, which last about as long as New Year's resolutions. Insight is the beginning of therapy, not the end goal. Our job as clinicians is to remind trauma clients, firmly but gently, that others have transcended, found hope, and derived meaning. They can as well.

Ask clients to construct a vision of where they would like to be within five years of recovery and how they would see themselves with (relative) freedom from fear. What do they envision themselves doing? What is their personal vision of meaning? These simple questions can yield powerful results. Posing these questions—even at times you would expect the client not to hear you—can have a lasting, salutary effect. I try to remind clients of the teleological part of their recovery with great frequency. I have raised these questions during times of "meltdown," relapse, triggering, or less dramatic regression. It is amazing how often clients will remember these questions years later and report that they somehow helped them transcend the crisis.

Clinical Principle 8: Unmasking the Inner Voice

I do not mystify the process of the inner voice, as has been the tradition of psychoanalysis. I tend to make it more concrete, along the lines of cognitive-behavioral tradition. I teach clients that they, just like the rest of us, have many little voices internally telling them and coaching them on a daily basis. Injured people may have more voices, hidden voices, and contradictory voices; this is completely normal. In fact, advise clients that the smarter they are, the more likely they engage multiple voices at multiple levels of awareness. However, the truly enlightened survivor learns to identify these voices and choose what messages to utilize.

Finally, it is important to remind clients that the destructive inner voices can use two languages: the language of relapse ("I really want to get high for the sake of getting high") or the language of self-invalidation ("I really don't deserve feeling good" or "I am really not worthy because I really know I am to blame").

Exposing these inner voices is a key component of therapy and recovery. Taking away the voices' power is vital. However, the goal is not to silence them. It is okay to hear, feel, and process doubt and negativity. The goal is not to "kill off" skeptical, fear-based, or warrior-based parts of the client's being but to simply "identify the hidden codes." In so doing, the client is not as likely to react in a fugue state, responding to anger, fear, and dissociation. By simply identifying the hidden messages and language of inner voices, clients become "co-therapists" in the quest to disentangle the inner chaos.

Contradictory and unconscious distortions need to be brought to the surface as quickly and safely as possible. This can be challenging, and waiting for clients to derive certain insights can take too much time. I often say to trauma clients, "Grieve the ideal; celebrate the real." The goal is not to simply remind the client to be grateful. The objective is identifying, demystifying, and articulating a powerful inner dynamic.

Clients with trauma disorders tend to cling to an idealized set of self-expectations. They believe that in order to feel safe, the world around them needs to meet unrealistically high expectations. On the one hand, trauma clients tend to be nihilistic, expecting the worst. Simultaneously, trauma clients aspire to a perfect world and a perfect self. It is as if perfection will make everything manageable and safe. Although such perfection is clearly an illusion, clients need to become more aware when they engage in this type of distortion.

Reciting this shortcut to the unconscious—*"Grieve the ideal; celebrate the real"*—facilitates a here-and-now focus. Recitation of this simple phrase, especially when clients become hypercritical or cynical, can redirect them back to the therapy process. It also serves to interrupt a nihilistic inner dynamic. With the split consciousness that is normal for complex survivors, they are often not fully present, especially in the therapy setting. By reminding and reciting the above theme, the clinician can avoid the exhausting repetition of hearing why the client is angry. Validating the anger is okay, but reinforcing their dwelling on their anger is not productive.

Also noteworthy is that when this shortcut is introduced to clients, they quickly discern that you, the clinician, understand their innermost themes. This is especially true if you explain to them that this phrase is a reminder that they need to not engage in behaviors that thrive on unattainable, idealistic, contradictory, and nihilistic distortions. This is really not as complicated as it sounds. You gain incredible credibility when clients know that you understand them. However, do not fall prey to the seduction of being the omniscient mystic. Mysticism builds dependency and slows down skill building. I emphasize a compassionate, insightful process of simplification, not mystification. Surprisingly, the clinician actually gains power, respect, and credibility by displaying this level of rapid awareness followed by a humble, nonmystical declaration. This is why I recommend using key phrases that simplify complex, self-destructive inner processes.

Clinical Principle 9: Reinforce the Observer Self

Clinicians are external observers interpreting past and current events. We have the advantage of objectivity, rationality, and clarity. A powerful clinical technique for clients with trauma-based disorders is to actively teach them to develop an observer self, sometimes referred to as an observer superego. The task is quite straightforward. Teach the client to think as an objective observer of his or her past and current reality. The observer self has been described in psychodynamic literature, but I am using the descriptive label in the cognitive-behavioral tradition. I actively encourage clients to become better observers of self or, to put it in behavioral terms, better "self-scientists."

As clinicians, we have an objectivity and distance from the clients' emotionally driven perception; this is what permits us to assist them. If we felt what they felt, we would be incapacitated rather quickly. This is why clinicians need to be careful about secondary traumatization, a real hazard in working with survivors. If we lose our objectivity, we lose our ability to help. Conversely, if we become dissociated, our highly intuitive and very sensitive clients easily detect our lack of empathy. Thus, we must find and remain in that middle ground: caring and detached. Harry Stack Sullivan's description of "the participant-observer" is a close approximation.

Explain to clients how you are hoping to assist them to see themselves with greater clarity and objectivity. I teach clients simple VKD-type skills, asking them to see themselves as if they were watching a movie screen or operating a video camera. This skill permits clients to observe, not dissociate. It facilitates choice and objectivity, the very skill set so desperately needed. In addition, I tell clients that it is normal to remember traumatic events as if they were seeing them through their own eyes. Victims tend to recall the past in this fashion. However, those who get healthier tend to see the event(s) as if they were watching a movie or television show.

Note that use of the observer self is a key component of several hypnotic techniques, including those oriented toward pain management. These techniques teach the client to observe traumatic events through the observer self and then ask the client to declare, "I am watching what happened to me in the past, and now at this point in my life I am strong enough and have enough supports to protect myself. I intend not to let anything like this happen again. I will use all my best judgment and resources to keep me safe."

Clinical Principle 10: Four-Dimensional Commentary, Repetition of the Basics, and the Power of Summary

When working with trauma clients, it is helpful to methodically think in terms of the four key dimensions: biological, psychological, interpersonal, and spiritual. (Review figure 7 from chapter 4.) Clinicians should listen carefully for issues and symptoms connected to each of these dimensions. It is easy to lose sight of these interconnected factors, so I encourage the clinician to visualize the four-dimensional grid before each session. Systematic inquiry about each of these dimensions, especially early in the therapy process, reinforces a methodical examination of each of these powerful factors. Clients can be triggered in one dimension, but all of the dimensions are affected.

Clients can also benefit from the use of this multidimensional process. They can learn to examine the impact of an event or memory in terms of the four critical dimensions. As a result, clients learn to use multiple techniques to work through emotions, memories, and triggers. The greater their perceptual clarity, and the more they seek to understand all of the factors and dimensions, the more empowered they become as "self-scientists." Real progress with trauma-based clients tends to require methodical and repeated work in all four critical areas. To focus on only one factor, especially early in therapy, can impede progress and undermine the therapeutic process.

I have learned that it is vital to repeat suggestions to clients with trauma disorders. This is not a reflection of their intellect, but rather a reflection of the cognitive and emotional "noise" they must contend with. Repetition increases the likelihood of your comments being heard. Many clinicians, especially those with analytic training, tend to say something once during a session, assuming the client must process, embrace, and incorporate what the clinician has said. I have found that if I say it only once, it may not get heard. Therefore, I tend to repeat most of what I have suggested to the client during the session. This applies to key insights, not just suggested changes in behavior.

Summaries are inherently soothing. They indicate to clients that they have been heard. In addition, the clinician's summary of what was covered, discovered, processed, learned, and suggested really helps soothe the fear of the client. The better the clinician becomes at the art of summary, the more powerful the therapeutic impact. Trauma-based clients, particularly those with addictive disorders, appreciate clarity of vision, coupled with objectivity. Summary statements during the course of the therapy hour can be more valuable than any brilliant comment, insight, or technique. Summary statements of all four dimensions provide an incredibly simple and powerful means of teaching clients better skills of observation and permit the necessary freedom from emotionality to move forward in therapy. Clarity and objectivity are antidotes to the intense, limbic intrusions that trauma clients tend to endure. Summary statements also role-model applied integration: The clinician pulls together the larger picture, and this soothes, enlightens, and teaches integration skills.

Clinical Principle 11: Dynamic Interpretation

Dynamic interpretation is not as complicated or mystical as it might sound. There are a number of fairly universal dynamic questions the clinician can ask a client. In the following list, most of the questions deal with the demystification of triggers.

1. How did what happened today remind you of what went wrong years ago, when ________ (name traumatic event) occurred?
2. Did the person whom you saw today or who set you off today in any way remind you of ________ (name the perpetrator)?

3. You mentioned that you felt a sudden surge of rage. Can you identify exactly who or what set that off? Do you notice any pattern in terms of when you are more likely to have this happen?
4. What are the patterns involved? (Keep in mind anniversary dates, a subtle trigger.)
5. It sounds like you were reaffirming your sexual identity by behaving as you did. Are you aware of how that might be connected to your abuse history?
6. It sounds like you were being provocative (or seductive, argumentative, rebellious, impulsive). Is this related to your past?
7. Where are you in terms of making peace with the warrior part of you? Are you having difficulty letting go of that?
8. It sounds like you might have unconsciously let chaos call you again. Can you tell me what might have set that dynamic back into motion?
9. Were your choices today empowering, or were they part of the old pattern of repetitive/compulsive self-invalidating behavior?
10. Can you tell me who was in your head or what memories or intrusions might have resulted in your becoming fearful? (If the clinician knows the answer, he or she might instead ask, "It sounds like you were hearing _______ [the perpetrator] telling you that little girls are bad. We know that this sets off an internal chain reaction. How did it work today?")
11. Some survivors act out in ways that are similar to the perpetrator. When you lost your composure with _______ (name the person), were you acting as if you were your perpetrator, Mom, Dad, or someone else?
12. Your sleep has been disrupted lately and you apparently are eating lots of sugar and caffeine. Is this related to your core history; have you been triggered; or is this part of that self-punishment dynamic we have seen before? You realize that letting go of that tendency is difficult and many survivors don't see it coming. I want to help you see it and then learn to interrupt it before it actually takes hold. This is similar to what you learned about relapse prevention, but it applies to your abuse, as well as that ongoing tendency for you to set yourself up for chaos, rejection, or harm.

13. You've been telling me that your back has been hurting and your neck is sore. Some survivors experience body memories. Is there any connection with these symptoms and what happened to you long ago?
14. It seems that you are isolating more and more, and that you are going to fewer meetings. Most times this would look like a potential relapse for your chemical. It could also be that you have been triggered in some way and that rather than wanting to use, maybe you are returning to behaviors that make you feel worse. Is your isolation connected to old feelings, or is it that you want to use, or both?
15. It seems like you have become more anxious, perfectionist, and demanding. Is this connected in any way to the traumatic events of the past? Are the old shadows part of this? Is your arrogance a function of being triggered?
16. You keep complaining about everyone's faults. In the program we say you are taking others' inventories. I am wondering if this is the victim variant of terminal uniqueness? What do you think? Is there a connection? As you might remember, I have found many survivors in early recovery vacillate between shame and arrogance. What's been going on with you since we met last?

Dynamic interpretation is a clinical art form. It really takes careful listening and synthesis for the clinician to perform. However, there are some reliable themes for which the clinician needs to remind the client. Our goal is not simply insight, nor are we seeking the mystical "aha" awakening. Dynamic interpretation, in my opinion, is really the core of trigger analysis. It reinforces the self-scientist/objective observer. The goal is not insight for the sake of insight. Rather, the client needs to become more skilled at recognizing when old themes or painful issues from the past contaminate thinking and perception. Since trauma tends to remain as part of the daily consciousness of the survivor, recognizing how it contaminates reality is a vital part of "working through," a key in the process of therapy.

Finally, let me remind the clinician that you need not be a genius, guru, or wizard. You don't need to figure out precisely how the client's themes and issues fit together. You simply need to prompt the client to look for his or her own answers. We don't make the actual connections; we just create the opportunity and facilitate a difficult process.

Some young clinicians take on the challenge of dynamic interpretation too literally and out of context. We are not tasked with finding the missing link and figuring out why it all hurts. Let go of the fantasy that you will see what the client misses. The big breakthroughs occur with our asking questions more often than with us linking together the missing pieces. Insight is an inside job. We are simply the facilitators.

Clinical Principle 12: Beware of Clinician Heliocentrism and Client Splitting

Heliocentrism is the notion that the universe revolves around the sun. Indeed the Earth revolves around the sun, but the universe does not. Modern science corrected this long-held perceptual flaw. Our sun is one of many in a much more complex universe than we imagined a few centuries ago. Initially, the individual clinician becomes the center of the client's universe, and this is particularly true for clients with trauma-based disorders. Clinicians, if they are not careful, can easily be influenced by the client's perception that the clinician is the center of the client's universe.

One of the great hazards of working with trauma-disorder clients is the powerful impact of their issues upon clinicians. An entire book could be devoted to this topic, and indeed, many articles and books address the general issues of countertransference or clinician's emotional reactions to their clients. More than in most endeavors, the clinician's emotional grounding, balance, and clarity of judgment are vital in terms of the work we do. It is not easy to hear some of what we hear, and loss of objectivity is an ongoing struggle. One of the biggest hazards is clinicians falling prey to the illusion that they are the saviors or rescuers of highly distressed, volatile, and incredibly needy clients. Trauma-disorder clients tend to put considerable pressure on clinicians. They reinforce the notion that others have betrayed them and that the clinician is their last hope. Whereas there may be elements of truth to this, the desperation generated by these clients can easily distort the clinician's judgment and boundary systems. Trauma-disorder clients, especially those with CPTSD (mislabeled, in my opinion, as borderline personality disorder), bring enormous intensity into the clinical process. These clients personalize everything, engage in many manipulations, and are desperately needy. I have seen many clinicians lose their moorings as a result of the client's intensity and neediness. One of the most common consequences is the narrowing of clinical vision. Specifically, the clinician can begin to think that he or she is the only link in this client's survival. There may be some validity to this notion, but accepting the full burden can be a setup.

Some clinicians begin to think that they are unique, gifted, and special. Trauma-based clients, especially those with CPTSD, are likely to say: "You are the only one who understands me. You are the only one who has helped me." Again, there may be some truth in this statement, but it is mostly a setup for loss of objectivity. A clinician can begin thinking in a fashion similar to that of the client. The clinician's internal dialogue may sound like this: "This client has been misunderstood by everyone else. He or she has been blamed for his or her symptoms and misjudged. Only I see the truth, and I am the only buffer from complete disaster. The client has told me things that nobody has ever heard before. I must work harder to maintain this trust, and I must protect the client from naive people who just don't understand. In addition, my training, background, and understanding are unique. Nobody can do what I am doing. My training is unique and my belief system, approach, technique, and clinical model are the only ones that work."

Accepting the illusion that you are the only one who understands has many hazards. It tends to reinforce isolation and overemphasizes the power of individual therapy.

I am a strong, strong believer in individual psychotherapy; I have decades of experience in this endeavor and believe in its necessity. However, with trauma-based disorders, we are dealing with clients who trust few and wish to stay isolated. If we become part of this dynamic, we are vulnerable to the same illusion that keeps the client ill. This illusion is perhaps why the individual therapy model tends to fail so often with dual disorder clients. It may also be why the literature states that people with borderline personality disorder are untreatable. Indeed, most clients with complex PTSD cannot be successfully treated individually. They need more. Individual psychotherapy is the beginning, and it is simply part of a larger process. The therapeutic bond is a tool to help trauma clients reconnect with other supports. The clinician should not remain the center of the client's universe.

The goal of therapy is to reconnect individuals to larger, healthier support systems. We facilitate personal as well as social reintegration. However, we can easily be misguided by the power and attractiveness of being the center of another's universe. Clinicians can lose their objectivity and fail to utilize the multiple supports and therapeutic systems available to them.

I discovered that even though I was a skilled individual clinician, I could not alone treat the most traumatized clients, especially those with co-occurring addictions. More structure, different levels of care, and more intensity were needed than an individual could ever provide. The individual clinician must reinforce the use of a formal or informal team system. Complex clients need multiple healers and often benefit from multiple approaches. Individual clinicians cannot provide all of this. We must use other experts and supports, fully engaging the multidimensional approaches that can assist these clients. Do not hesitate to use multidisciplinary community resources, such as AA or NA, psychiatrists, relapse prevention groups, trauma-support groups (preferably with professional support), nutritional consultants, or clergy members. Integrate a support team using the best resources of your community. It takes more than an individual to treat this population, and the intensity varies with the degree of distress.

In some instances, higher levels of care may be needed. This is not an indication of failure, but simply a reflection of client intensity. In some instances, inpatient stabilization is vital followed by varying levels of structured residential care. Too often, clients with complex issues are sent home after primary addiction treatment. Some are sent to halfway houses with little structure, therapy, or clinical sophistication. The general error is too little therapy. Some of the most compelling clients also benefit from a change in setting. The "geographic cure" has been derided in some circles, but for the complex client in need of multiple interventions, it can make a huge therapeutic contribution.

Use multiple systems and multiple strategies. Be prepared to let clients move to different levels of care, based upon their need not our codependency. Weave together a local team with whom you can cover all the therapeutic dimensions, and know the resources for higher levels of care. Trauma-disorder clients need an ongoing team approach. Do not strive to be a superstar when a team effort is almost always needed.

Client splitting is another part of what can be expected in the therapeutic process. The client unconsciously manipulates the therapist into believing that everyone has been mean-spirited or is incompetent. The client seeks unconditional support, and this places the well-intended clinician in a bind. If the clinician is part of an integrated system, the client, especially the more distressed client, may try to separate or "split" the clinician from his or her support systems. Splitting is often seen in very negative terms, but in essence, it is really the client, or his or her pathology, doing what is intuitive. Splitting is not a conscious, malevolent endeavor in most instances. As one supervisee stated: "If I support the client, I am feeding victim thinking. If I challenge the client, he or she will see me as rejecting." The hazards of feeding victim thinking tend to outweigh the hazards of perceived rejection. I have found it most helpful to be direct, sometimes humorous, and occasionally ironic.

One very difficult client told me that one member of the treatment team in our setting was confronting him with consequences and was "being mean." He referred to the therapist, whom he had trusted completely a few weeks earlier, as "Captain Bligh." I said to this very complex client, "That's really odd. You liked your therapist until today. I wonder what set off that sudden shift. You know that when trauma survivors go through those sudden shifts, it is a clue that they might have been triggered. Now, I was not there, so I can't objectively state whether your therapist was being mean. However, I suspect that other issues may be involved. I am suspicious that perhaps something happened so that you now see him the way you used to see your father. It seems like anyone with authority can be seen as untrustworthy if you get triggered. Is there any connection here?" I then paused and let the client respond.

In this instance, the client immediately agreed with my interpretation but went on to complain: "Well maybe he did seem like my father, but he still became Captain Bligh."

"Well maybe he was less-than-perfectly attuned to what was going on," I said. "Perhaps you and he and I should confer so that we can clear up the confusion. You know that my knowing how he triggered you is useless unless you spread the wealth. He needs to understand you better as well. So, how about you try to tell him, and if you run into trouble, I can help you. If you want, I can tell him what we discovered before you tell him directly. Whatever makes you most comfortable is fine with me."

This type of clinical response interrupts the splitting process and reinforces the major mission: The client needs to understand, communicate, interrupt victim process, and share insights outside of the individual therapy situation. In the instance cited, the crisis was interrupted, the splitting disengaged, and the client saw his distortions at work. We not only gained insight but also interrupted a potentially dangerous split. My final feedback to this client was humorous, but true: "By the way, you referred to your therapist as Captain Bligh. Did you know that Captain Bligh may have actually been a victim of historical distortion? A recent history book that looked at the story (and movie) of *Mutiny on the Bounty* and the author, Caroline Alexander, indicated that Captain Bligh was an amazing sailor who pulled off one of the most incredible feats of individual seamanship ever recorded. Despite how he was portrayed in the movie, Bligh might have been the victim of an unjust mutiny. Bligh apparently was a hero and a brilliant sailor. I'm not saying I know for sure what the complete story was, but Bligh may not have been the evildoer portrayed in the movies and fictionalized accounts. So, you might have been complimenting your therapist without realizing it."

Internal integration is the goal of therapy with trauma-related disorders. Team cohesion is another part of this integration process. Beware of splitting. It is a common part of the dynamic brought forth by trauma-disorder clients.

Another hazard of splitting or the unconscious manipulations that reflect victim dynamics, expressed by "everyone is against me, except maybe you," is that the client may demand certain boundary tests for the clinician. The client may say, "If you really do care, and you really are going to save me, then you must demonstrate it by ________________ (the terms of the boundary violation)."

Again, a whole book can be devoted to the transference/countertransference process, but a final, simple rule must be reiterated: Never, ever violate the basic rules of the clinical professions. There are no exceptions. The desperation generated by trauma-disorder clients puts extra pressure on many clinicians. Always stay within the rules. It is in your best interest as well as the client's. Do not go out on the edge. Clinicians must stay balanced and healthy. We can care, but we must never engage in any behavior that bends the rules. This is true for all kinds of clients, but it is particularly true for trauma-based disorders.

■ ■ ■

EPILOGUE

My goal for this book was to articulate a first step toward improved services for survivors. I endeavored to present a simple yet meaningful foundation for mental health and addiction counselors to better understand how these conditions work together. It is my hope that clinicians will be better equipped to recognize and intervene with addicts suffering from trauma-based disorders. I hope that readers will become integrative thinkers, less likely to be seduced by simple answers to complex problems. As articulated in these pages, the more intense the trauma, the more complex the client and, therefore, the more likely addiction will be part of the picture. I also hope that individuals with borderline personality disorder will be correctly seen for who they really are, complex survivors. Additionally, addressing the needs of survivors can make a huge contribution in preventing relapse.

My key theme, integration, is easy to state and difficult to achieve. A multimodal integrative approach is more than eclecticism. It requires considerable effort for clinicians and programs at all levels of care. The trend toward treating co-occurring disorders is a beginning.

Many providers and programs profess an integrated service model but cannot deliver. There is often a gap between what is intended and written in brochures or stated by providers. As we have learned with addicts, declarations do not matter unless actual behavior follows. Do your homework and know your providers. Good boundaries, integrity, and balanced judgment are essential. Rely on what is done, not simply what is declared.

If this book has shifted your perspective, given you new insight, or simply reinforced the good vision you had, I have achieved a goal. If you have a deeper understanding of trauma-related disorders, I have approximated a personal teleology. In the future, I intend to write more about teleology and the envisioning of long-term goals articulated by Frankl. This is an untapped part of the spiritual domain that is particularly helpful to addicted survivors.

I am hoping my multidimensional, integrated perspective will make more than a transitory impact. I am hoping that it will raise the bar for a higher standard of care. After all, survivors deserve the best synthesis we can articulate and deliver.

Finally, keep in mind that those who enter this field are on a spiritual journey. May we all continue to function as "gurus," bringing light where there was once darkness. May we do so with balance, sincerity, and clarity.

■ ■ ■

BIBLIOGRAPHY

AA World Services. 2001. *Alcoholics Anonymous.* 4th ed. New York: AA World Services.

Alexander, Caroline. 2003. *The Bounty: The True Story of the Mutiny on the Bounty.* New York: Viking Books.

American Psychiatric Association. 2000. *Diagnostic and Statistical Manual of Mental Disorders.* 4th ed. Washington, DC: American Psychiatric Association.

Fearless. 1993. DVD, directed by Peter Weir, Warner Home Video, released 1999.

Foa, Edna, Terence Keane, and Matthew Friedman. 2000. *Effective Treatments for PTSD: Practice Guidelines from the International Society for Traumatic Stress Studies.* New York: Guilford Press.

Frankl, Viktor E. 1984. *Man's Search for Meaning.* New York: Pocket Books.

Herman, Judith. 1997. *Trauma and Recovery.* New York: Basic Books.

Kroll, Jerome. 1993. *PTSD/Borderlines in Therapy: Finding the Balance.* New York: W. W. Norton & Company.

Lazarus, Arnold A. 1989. *The Practice of Multimodal Therapy: Systematic, Comprehensive, and Effective Psychotherapy.* Baltimore, MD: Johns Hopkins University Press.

Levine, Peter A. 1997. *Waking the Tiger: Healing Trauma.* Berkeley, CA: North Atlantic Books.

Linehan, Marsha M. 1993. *Cognitive-Behavioral Treatment of Borderline Personality Disorder.* New York: Guilford Press.

Millon, Theodore. 1983. *Modern Psychopathology: A Biosocial Approach to Maladaptive Learning and Functioning.* Prospect Heights, IL: Waveland Press.

Ogden, Pat, and Kekuni Minton. 2000. Sensorimotor Psychotherapy: One Method for Processing Traumatic Memory. *Traumatology* 6, no. 3 (October): 149–73.

Philpott, Tom. 2002. *Glory Denied: The Saga of Vietnam Veteran Jim Thompson, America's Longest-Held Prisoner of War.* New York: Plume.

Pitman, Roger K., Kathy M. Sanders, Randall M. Zusman, Anna R. Healy, Farah Cheema, Natasha B. Lasko, Larry Cahill, and Scott P. Orr. 2002. Pilot Study of Secondary Prevention of Posttraumatic Stress Disorder with Propranolol. *Biological Psychiatry* 51, no. 2 (January 15): 189–92.

Ross, Colin. 2000. *The Trauma Model: A Solution to the Problem of Comorbidity in Psychiatry.* Richardson, TX: Manitou Communications.

Rothschild, Babette. 2000. *The Body Remembers: The Psychophysiology of Trauma and Trauma Treatment.* New York: W.W. Norton & Company.

Shapiro, Francine. 1995. *Eye Movement Desensitization and Reprocessing: Basic Principles, Protocols, and Procedures.* New York: Guilford Press.

Yalom, Irvin D. 1995. *The Theory and Practice of Group Psychotherapy.* 4th ed. New York: Basic Books.

———. 2000. *Love's Executioner: And Other Tales of Psychotherapy.* New York: Perennial.

Yehuda, Rachel. 1990. Low Urinary Cortisol Excretion in Patients with Post-traumatic Stress Disorder. *Journal of Nervous and Mental Diseases* 178, no. 6: 366–69.

Additional Readings

Catherall, Donald R. 2004. *The Handbook of Stress, Trauma, and the Family.* Philadelphia, PA: Brunner-Routledge.

Cole, Tom. 1983. *Medal of Honor Rag: A Full Length Play in One Act.* New York: S. French.

Courtois, Christine A. 1999. *Recollections of Sexual Abuse: Treatment Principles and Guidelines.* New York: W.W. Norton & Company.

Figley, Charles, ed. 1995. *Compassion Fatigue: Coping with Secondary Traumatic Stress Disorder in Those Who Treat the Traumatized.* New York: Brunner Mazel.

Friedrich, William N. 1990. *Psychotherapy of Sexually Abused Children and Their Families.* New York: W.W. Norton & Company.

Hedges, Chris. 2003. *War Is a Force That Gives Us Meaning.* New York: Anchor Books/Doubleday.

Kirschner, Sam, Diana Kirschner, and Richard Rappaport. 1993. *Working with Adult Incest Survivors: The Healing Journey.* New York: Brunner Mazel.

Lomax, Eric. 1996. *The Railway Man: A True Story of War, Remembrance, and Forgiveness.* New York: Ballantine Books.

Matsakis, Aphrodite. 1992. *I Can't Get Over It: A Handbook for Trauma Survivors.* Oakland, CA: New Harbinger Publications.

Meiselman, Karin C. 1990. *Resolving the Trauma of Incest: Reintegration Therapy with Survivors.* San Francisco: Jossey-Bass.

Sanders, Catherine M. 1989. *Grief: The Mourning After: Dealing with Adult Bereavement.* New York: John Wiley & Sons.

Shephard, Ben. 2001. *A War of Nerves: Soldiers and Psychiatrists in the Twentieth Century.* London: Jonathan Cape.

Stout, Martha. 2001. *The Myth of Sanity: Divided Consciousness and the Promise of Awareness.* Middlesex, England: Penguin Books.

Trimble, Michael R. 1981. *Post-traumatic Neurosis: From Railway Spine to the Whiplash.* New York: John Wiley & Sons.

Wilson, John P., Matthew J. Friedman, and Jacob D. Lindy. 2001. *Treating Psychological Trauma and PTSD.* New York: Guilford Press.

Additional Films

Antwone Fisher. 2002. DVD, directed by Denzel Washington. Twentieth Century Fox Home Entertainment, released 2003.

Apocalypse Now. 1979. DVD, directed by Francis Ford Coppola. Paramount, released 1999.

Behind the Lines. 1998. DVD, directed by Gillies MacKinnon. Artisan Entertainment, released 2003.

Good Will Hunting. 1997. DVD, directed by Gus van Sant. Miramax Home Entertainment, released 1999.

Mystic River. 2003. DVD, directed by Clint Eastwood. Warner Home Video, released 2004.

Saving Private Ryan. 1999. DVD, directed by Steven Spielberg. Dreamworks, released 1999.

Smoke Signals. 1998. DVD, directed by Chris Eyre. Miramax Home Entertainment, released 1999.

Web Sites

Advanced Recovery Center
www.arc-hope.com

David Baldwin's Trauma Information Pages
www.trauma-pages.com

International Society for Traumatic Stress Studies
www.istss.org

Jeff and Debra Jay: Interventionists
www.lovefirst.net

Medscape Psychiatry
www.medscape.com

National Center for Post-traumatic Stress Disorder
www.ncptsd.org

National Comorbidity Study
www.hcp.med.harvard.edu/ncs/

National Institute of Mental Health
www.nimh.nih.gov

National Institute on Drug Abuse
www.nida.nih.gov

Quackwatch
www.quackwatch.org

INDEX

ABOUT THE AUTHOR

Jerry A. Boriskin, Ph.D., C.A.S., began working with Vietnam veterans in 1979, just as PTSD entered the professional and general vocabulary. Clinical director of one of the first Vet Centers, he quickly developed an expertise in addictive disorders. He transitioned to private practice in Florida in 1986, working with a wide range of trauma survivors, particularly sexual abuse survivors. He also became a psychological consultant for Hanley-Hazelden in West Palm Beach, Florida, and continued as a consulting lecturer for the Hazelden Foundation. He developed one of the earliest extended residential treatment programs and in 1999 he co-founded Advanced Recovery Center in Delray Beach, Florida.

A passionate advocate for integrated treatment, Boriskin has a vision that predated the ongoing movement toward specialized and integrated treatment for co-occurring disorders, particularly those involving trauma. He is a licensed clinical psychologist and a certified addiction specialist.

The author welcomes correspondence from readers. He may be reached at:

Jerry A. Boriskin, Ph.D.
Advanced Recovery Center
1300 17th Avenue NW, Suite 200
Delray Beach, FL 33445
561-274-7417
jerryboriskin.com

Hazelden Publishing and Educational Services is a division of the Hazelden Foundation, a not-for-profit organization. Since 1949, Hazelden has been a leader in promoting the dignity and treatment of people afflicted with the disease of chemical dependency.

The mission of the foundation is to improve the quality of life for individuals, families, and communities by providing a national continuum of information, education, and recovery services that are widely accessible; to advance the field through research and training; and to improve our quality and effectiveness through continuous improvement and innovation.

Stemming from that, the mission of this division is to provide quality information and support to people wherever they may be in their personal journey—from education and early intervention, through treatment and recovery, to personal and spiritual growth.

Although our treatment programs do not necessarily use everything Hazelden publishes, our bibliotherapeutic materials support our mission and the Twelve Step philosophy upon which it is based. We encourage your comments and feedback.

The headquarters of the Hazelden Foundation are in Center City, Minnesota. Additional treatment facilities are located in Chicago, Illinois; Newberg, Oregon; New York, New York; Plymouth, Minnesota; and St. Paul, Minnesota. At these sites, we provide a continuum of care for men and women of all ages. Our Plymouth facility is designed specifically for youth and families.